SHADOW

PHILIPPE FRANCQ • JEAN VAN HAMME

9th CINEBOOK
The 9th Art Publisher

With the authors' consent, and in order not to upset our more sensitive readers,
certain illustrations of this edition of *Largo Winch* have been modified.
The original version of *Largo Winch* is published in French by Dupuis.

Original title: Shadow

Original edition: © Dupuis, 2002
by Francq & Van Hamme
www.dupuis.com
http://www.largowinch.com

English translation: © 2010 Cinebook Ltd

Translator: Luke Spear
Lettering and text layout: Imadjinn
Printed in Spain by Just Colour Graphic

This edition first published in Great Britain in 2011 by
Cinebook Ltd
56 Beech Avenue
Canterbury, Kent
CT4 7TA
www.cinebook.com

A CIP catalogue record for this book
is available from the British Library

ISBN 978-1-84918-075-7

9th CINEBOOK
The 9th Art Publisher

SIMON OVRONNAZ, LARGO WINCH'S BEST FRIEND, HAS BEEN HIRED TO PLAY THE ROLE OF MIKE SHADOW IN A TELEVISED SERIES FILMED IN SAN FRANCISCO: "GOLDEN GATE." THIS SERIES, PAINFUL TO WATCH FROM THE OUTSET, IS BEING PRODUCED BY W9, ONE OF THE NETWORKS DIVISION COMPANIES OF THE W GROUP.

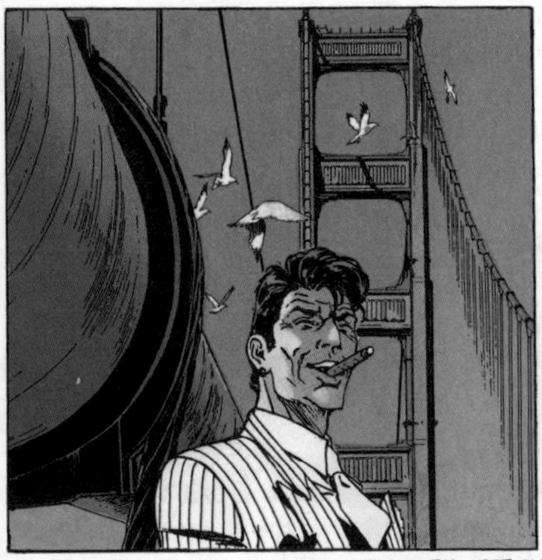

PRODUCED BY CANDID FILMS, AN INDEPENDENT PRODUCER FROM RENO, NEVADA, "GOLDEN GATE" HAS BEEN FINANCED BY A BACKER WHO WISHES TO REMAIN ANONYMOUS DUE TO THE $6-MILLION PRICE TAG PER EPISODE, WHICH IS MORE THAN FOUR TIMES THE NORM FOR A SERIES OF THIS KIND. BUT ONE OF THE CONTRACT'S CLAUSES STATES THAT HALF OF THIS FUNDING MUST BE TRANSFERRED BY W9 TO A SECRET ACCOUNT IN A BANK IN THE CAYMAN ISLANDS, WHICH IS ILLEGAL IF THE ACCOUNT HOLDER TURNS OUT TO BE AN AMERICAN CITIZEN.

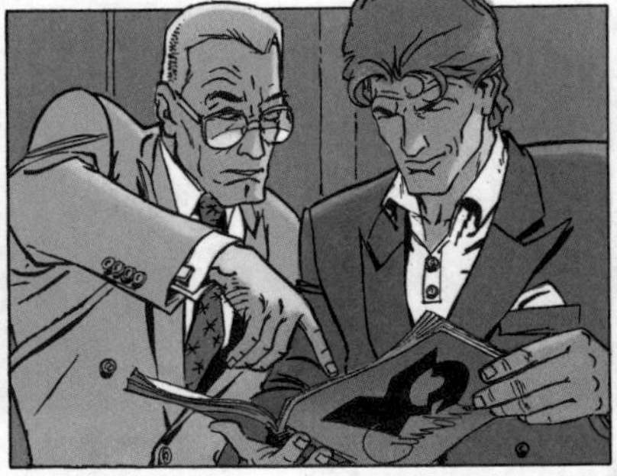

JUSTIFIABLY WORRIED, DWIGHT COCHRANE, THE W GROUP ADMINISTRATOR, HAS SENT ONE OF HIS INSPECTORS, SARAH WASHINGTON, TO FIND OUT MORE ON THE SCENE. BUT THE YOUNG WOMAN SEEMS TO HAVE DISAPPEARED. LARGO AND COCHRANE THEN DECIDE TO GO TO SAN FRANCISCO TO MEET NEW W9 DIRECTOR EARL QUINN, POACHED FROM NBN, A COMPETING NETWORK THAT BELONGS TO NED BAKER.

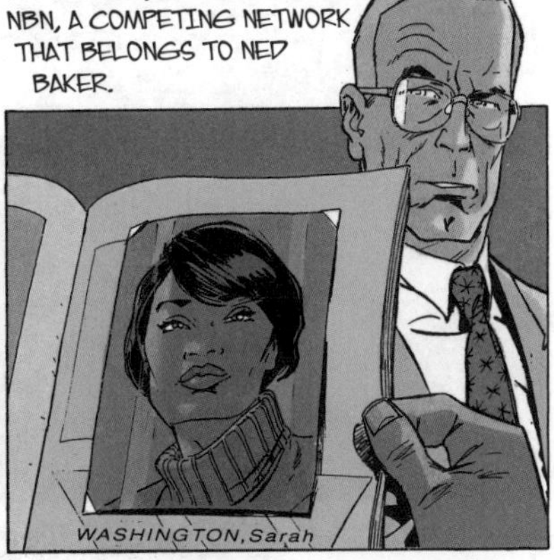
WASHINGTON,Sarah

SENSING SOME REALLY DIRTY FINANCIAL TRICKERY, LARGO WANTS TO HALT FILMING OF THE SERIES' 26 EPISODES. BUT QUINN WILL HAVE NONE OF IT. THE W9 ACCOUNTS ARE IN THE RED AND "GOLDEN GATE" REPRESENTS A UNIQUE OPPORTUNITY TO FILL THE NETWORK'S COFFERS ONCE AGAIN. FURTHERMORE, IF FILMING IS HALTED, W9 WILL HAVE TO REIMBURSE CANDID FILMS FOR $156 MILLION, PLUS A FEE OF $50 MILLION, WHICH IT CAN IN NO WAY AFFORD TO DO.

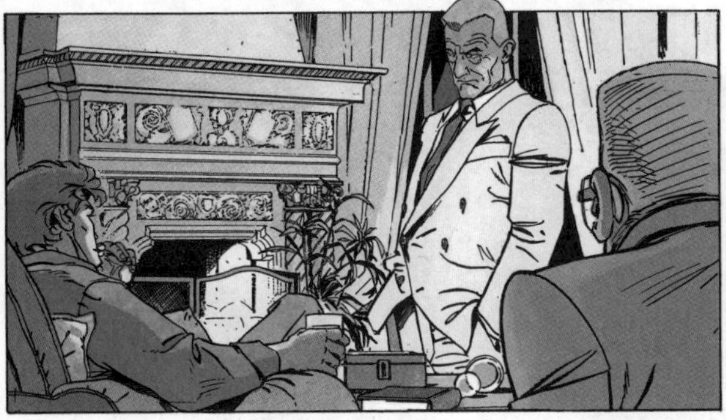

LARGO THUS DECIDES TO GO TO RENO TO SEE DON CANDIDO PANATELLA, THE CUBAN BOSS OF CANDID FILMS AND OWNER OF THE BIGGEST HOTEL-CASINO IN THE CITY. HE HEADS THERE IN THE COMPANY OF THE BEAUTIFUL FLOR DE LA CRUZ, DON CANDIDO'S ASSISTANT AND EXECUTIVE PRODUCER OF "GOLDEN GATE." BUT PANATELLA REFUSES TO REVEAL THE IDENTITY OF THE MYSTERIOUS SERIES BACKER.

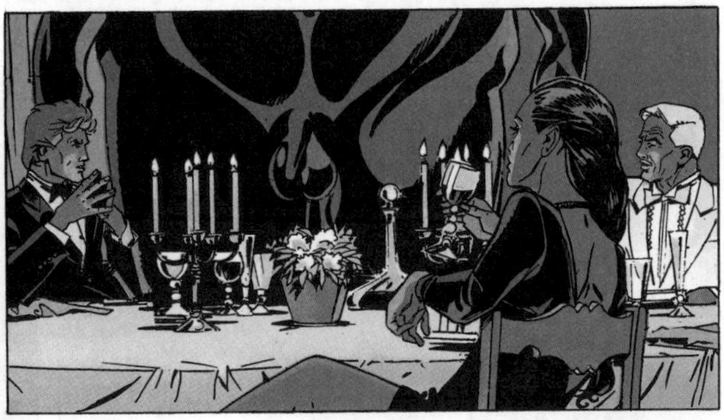

ON THE OTHER HAND, JULIET, A YOUNG HOSTESS HANDED TO HIM BY DON CANDIDO, REVEALS TO LARGO THAT HER BOSS RUNS A LARGE PROSTITUTION RING—OF WHICH SHE HERSELF IS A VICTIM. SHE BEGS HIM TO HELP HER ESCAPE. CHASED THROUGH THE DESERT BY PANATELLA'S HENCHMEN, LARGO AND JULIET MANAGE TO MAKE IT TO SAN FRANCISCO.

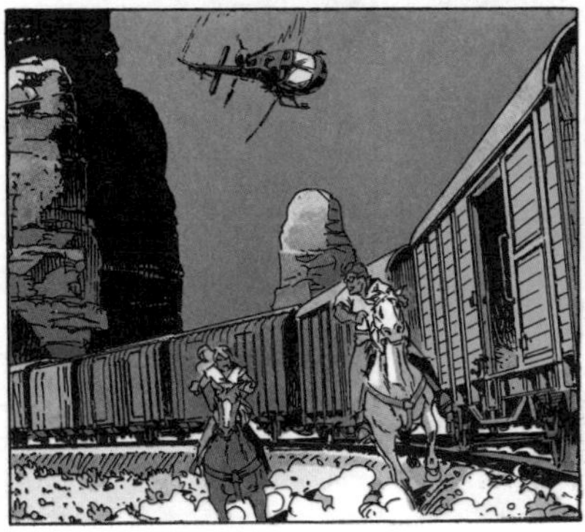

THIS IS WHERE A DOUBLE TWIST OCCURS. THE OWNER OF THE SECRET ACCOUNT IN THE CAYMAN ISLANDS TURNS OUT TO BE NONE OTHER THAN DWIGHT COCHRANE, AND LARGO IS ACCUSED OF HAVING ABDUCTED, CONFINED AND RAPED THE YOUNG JULIET, WHO IS A MINOR. WHILE THE NEWSPAPERS RUN THEIR BIG HEADLINES, THE TWO MEN ARE ARRESTED AND INCARCERATED.

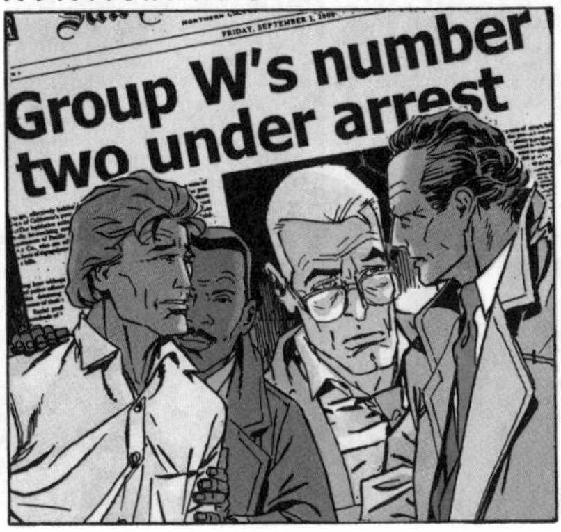
Group W's number two under arrest

ON THE TOP FLOOR OF THE GUANTANAMERA, DON CANDIDO'S HOTEL-CASINO IN RENO, PANATELLA, FLOR DE LA CRUZ, EARL QUINN AND NED BAKER CELEBRATE. THEIR PLAN HAS WORKED PERFECTLY, AND ALL THEY NEED TO DO NOW IS REAP THE REWARDS.

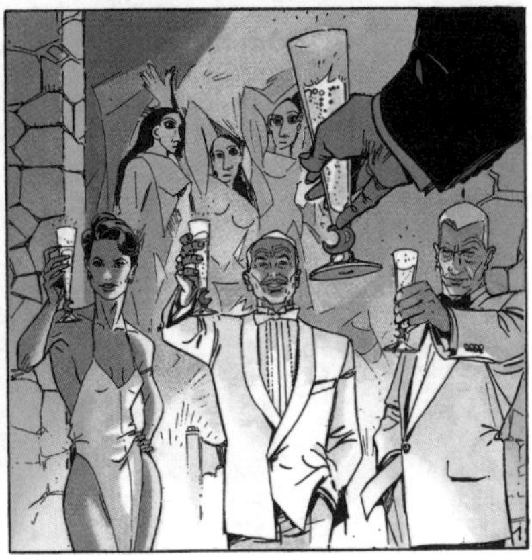

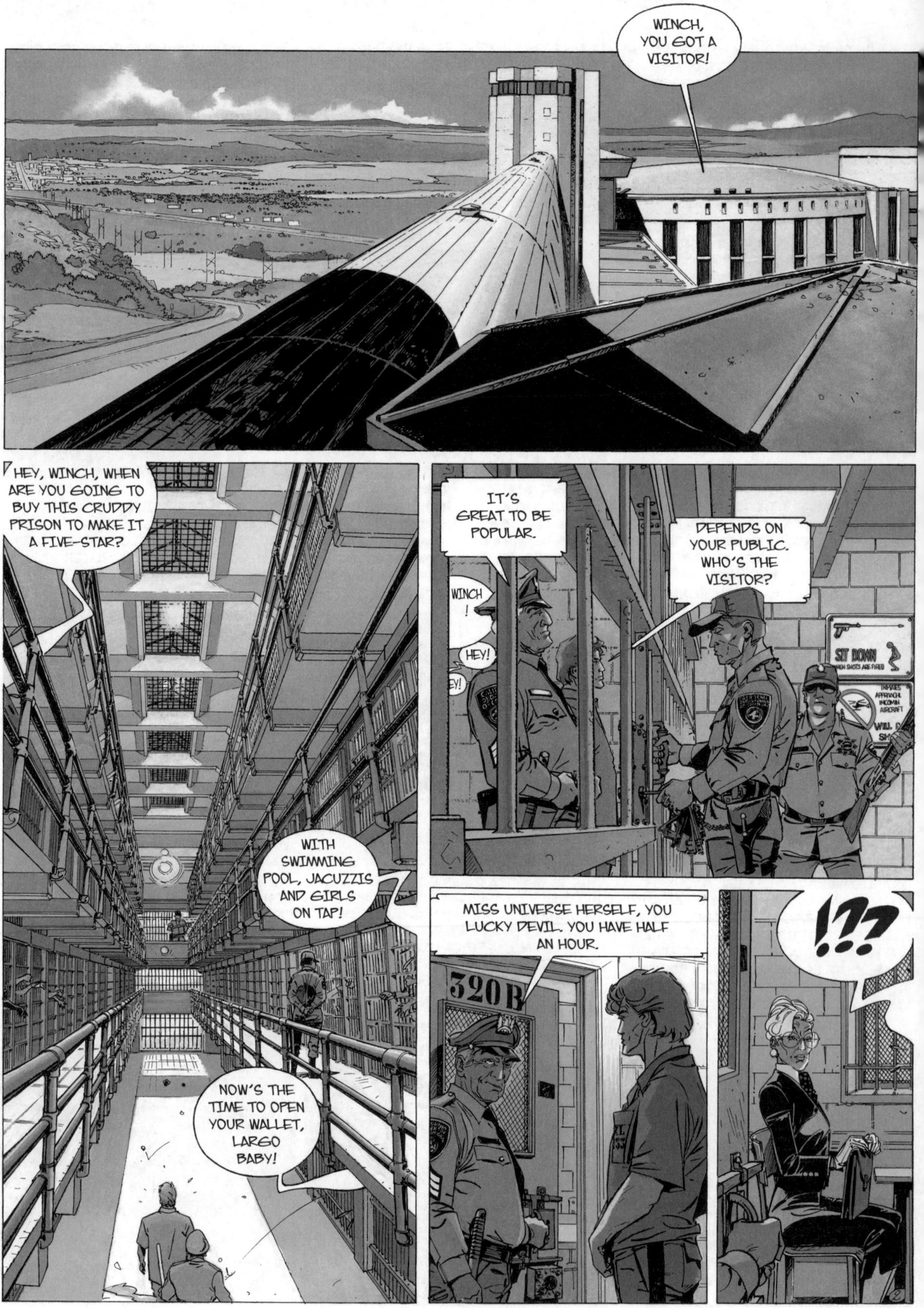

WINCH, YOU GOT A VISITOR!
HEY, WINCH, WHEN ARE YOU GOING TO BUY THIS CRUDDY PRISON TO MAKE IT A FIVE-STAR?
WITH SWIMMING POOL, JACUZZIS AND GIRLS ON TAP!
NOW'S THE TIME TO OPEN YOUR WALLET, LARGO BABY!
IT'S GREAT TO BE POPULAR.
WINCH !
HEY!
DEPENDS ON YOUR PUBLIC. WHO'S THE VISITOR?
SIT DOWN
MISS UNIVERSE HERSELF, YOU LUCKY DEVIL. YOU HAVE HALF AN HOUR.
320B
!??

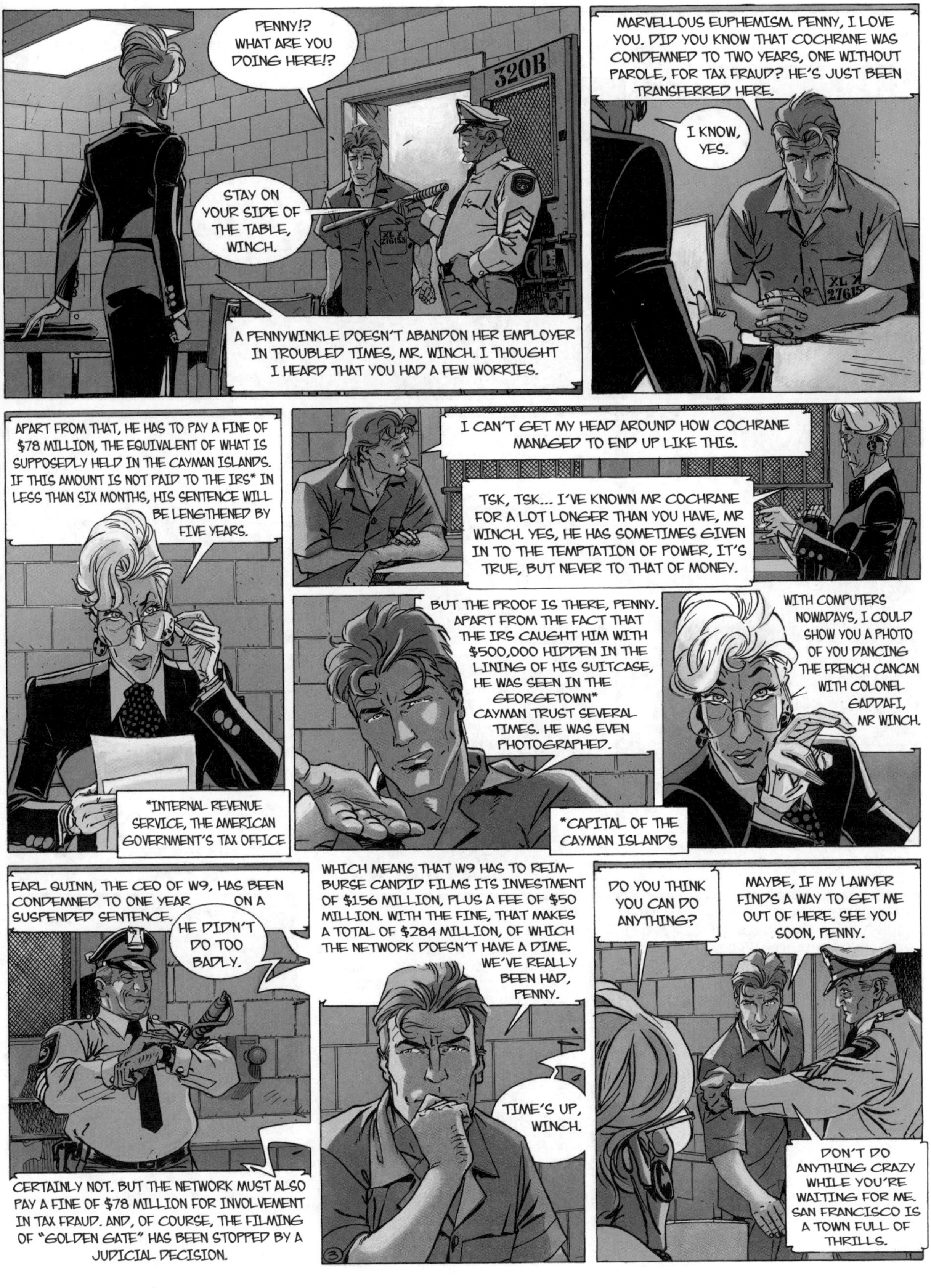

PENNY!? WHAT ARE YOU DOING HERE!?
STAY ON YOUR SIDE OF THE TABLE, WINCH.
A PENNYWINKLE DOESN'T ABANDON HER EMPLOYER IN TROUBLED TIMES, MR. WINCH. I THOUGHT I HEARD THAT YOU HAD A FEW WORRIES.
MARVELLOUS EUPHEMISM. PENNY, I LOVE YOU. DID YOU KNOW THAT COCHRANE WAS CONDEMNED TO TWO YEARS, ONE WITHOUT PAROLE, FOR TAX FRAUD? HE'S JUST BEEN TRANSFERRED HERE.
I KNOW, YES.
APART FROM THAT, HE HAS TO PAY A FINE OF $78 MILLION, THE EQUIVALENT OF WHAT IS SUPPOSEDLY HELD IN THE CAYMAN ISLANDS. IF THIS AMOUNT IS NOT PAID TO THE IRS* IN LESS THAN SIX MONTHS, HIS SENTENCE WILL BE LENGTHENED BY FIVE YEARS.
*INTERNAL REVENUE SERVICE, THE AMERICAN GOVERNMENT'S TAX OFFICE
I CAN'T GET MY HEAD AROUND HOW COCHRANE MANAGED TO END UP LIKE THIS.
TSK, TSK... I'VE KNOWN MR COCHRANE FOR A LOT LONGER THAN YOU HAVE, MR WINCH. YES, HE HAS SOMETIMES GIVEN IN TO THE TEMPTATION OF POWER, IT'S TRUE, BUT NEVER TO THAT OF MONEY.
BUT THE PROOF IS THERE, PENNY. APART FROM THE FACT THAT THE IRS CAUGHT HIM WITH $500,000 HIDDEN IN THE LINING OF HIS SUITCASE, HE WAS SEEN IN THE GEORGETOWN* CAYMAN TRUST SEVERAL TIMES. HE WAS EVEN PHOTOGRAPHED.
*CAPITAL OF THE CAYMAN ISLANDS
WITH COMPUTERS NOWADAYS, I COULD SHOW YOU A PHOTO OF YOU DANCING THE FRENCH CANCAN WITH COLONEL GADDAFI, MR WINCH.
EARL QUINN, THE CEO OF W9, HAS BEEN CONDEMNED TO ONE YEAR ON A SUSPENDED SENTENCE.
HE DIDN'T DO TOO BADLY.
CERTAINLY NOT. BUT THE NETWORK MUST ALSO PAY A FINE OF $78 MILLION FOR INVOLVEMENT IN TAX FRAUD. AND, OF COURSE, THE FILMING OF "GOLDEN GATE" HAS BEEN STOPPED BY A JUDICIAL DECISION.
WHICH MEANS THAT W9 HAS TO REIMBURSE CANDID FILMS ITS INVESTMENT OF $156 MILLION, PLUS A FEE OF $50 MILLION. WITH THE FINE, THAT MAKES A TOTAL OF $284 MILLION, OF WHICH THE NETWORK DOESN'T HAVE A DIME.
WE'VE REALLY BEEN HAD, PENNY.
TIME'S UP, WINCH.
DO YOU THINK YOU CAN DO ANYTHING?
MAYBE, IF MY LAWYER FINDS A WAY TO GET ME OUT OF HERE. SEE YOU SOON, PENNY.
DON'T DO ANYTHING CRAZY WHILE YOU'RE WAITING FOR ME. SAN FRANCISCO IS A TOWN FULL OF THRILLS.

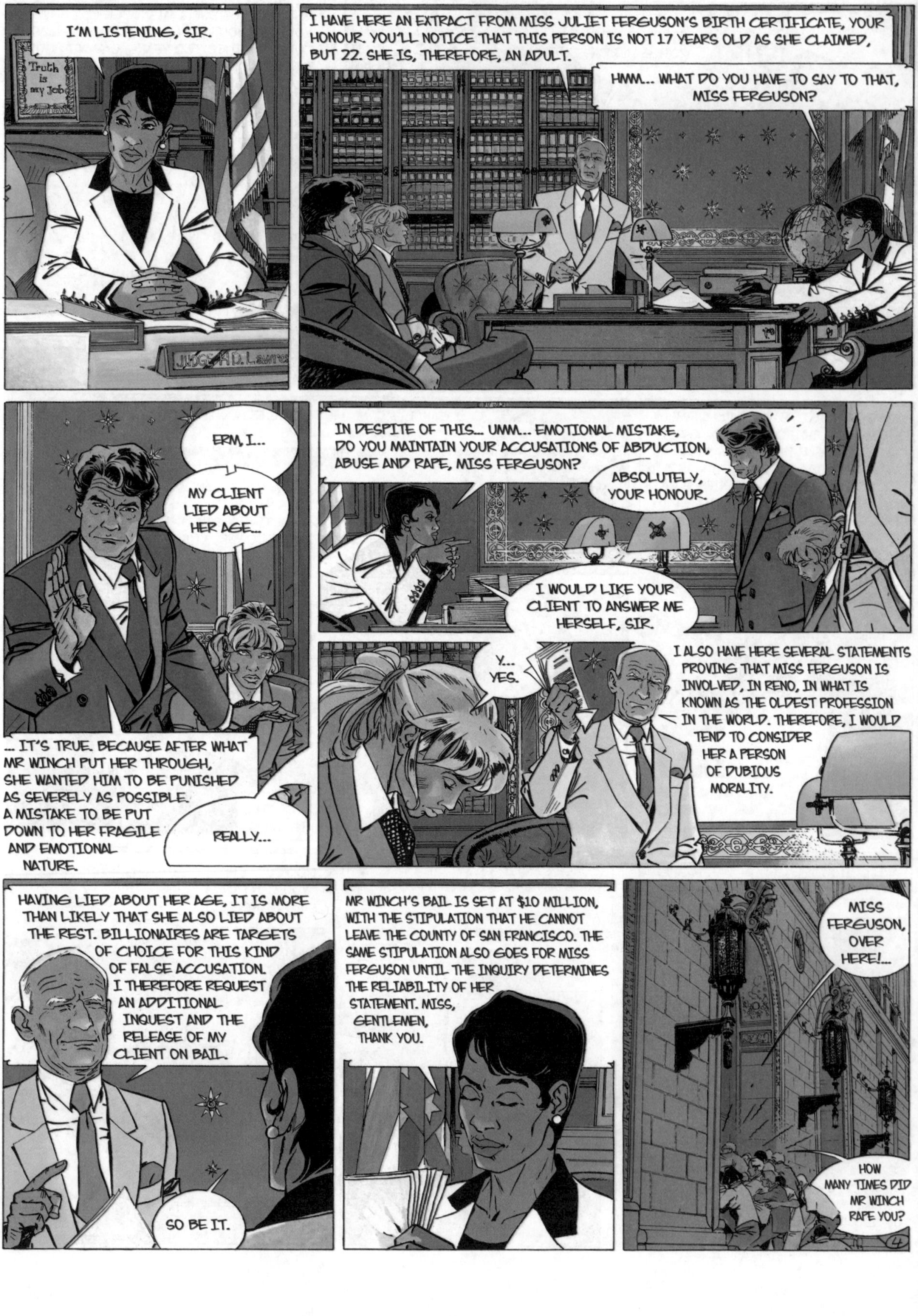

I'M LISTENING, SIR.
Truth is my Job
JUDGE H.D. Lawre
I HAVE HERE AN EXTRACT FROM MISS JULIET FERGUSON'S BIRTH CERTIFICATE, YOUR HONOUR. YOU'LL NOTICE THAT THIS PERSON IS NOT 17 YEARS OLD AS SHE CLAIMED, BUT 22. SHE IS, THEREFORE, AN ADULT.
HMM... WHAT DO YOU HAVE TO SAY TO THAT, MISS FERGUSON?
ERM, I...
MY CLIENT LIED ABOUT HER AGE...
... IT'S TRUE. BECAUSE AFTER WHAT MR WINCH PUT HER THROUGH, SHE WANTED HIM TO BE PUNISHED AS SEVERELY AS POSSIBLE. A MISTAKE TO BE PUT DOWN TO HER FRAGILE AND EMOTIONAL NATURE.
REALLY...
IN DESPITE OF THIS... UMM... EMOTIONAL MISTAKE, DO YOU MAINTAIN YOUR ACCUSATIONS OF ABDUCTION, ABUSE AND RAPE, MISS FERGUSON?
ABSOLUTELY, YOUR HONOUR.
I WOULD LIKE YOUR CLIENT TO ANSWER ME HERSELF, SIR.
Y... YES.
I ALSO HAVE HERE SEVERAL STATEMENTS PROVING THAT MISS FERGUSON IS INVOLVED, IN RENO, IN WHAT IS KNOWN AS THE OLDEST PROFESSION IN THE WORLD. THEREFORE, I WOULD TEND TO CONSIDER HER A PERSON OF DUBIOUS MORALITY.
HAVING LIED ABOUT HER AGE, IT IS MORE THAN LIKELY THAT SHE ALSO LIED ABOUT THE REST. BILLIONAIRES ARE TARGETS OF CHOICE FOR THIS KIND OF FALSE ACCUSATION. I THEREFORE REQUEST AN ADDITIONAL INQUEST AND THE RELEASE OF MY CLIENT ON BAIL.
SO BE IT.
MR WINCH'S BAIL IS SET AT $10 MILLION, WITH THE STIPULATION THAT HE CANNOT LEAVE THE COUNTY OF SAN FRANCISCO. THE SAME STIPULATION ALSO GOES FOR MISS FERGUSON UNTIL THE INQUIRY DETERMINES THE RELIABILITY OF HER STATEMENT. MISS, GENTLEMEN, THANK YOU.
MISS FERGUSON, OVER HERE!...
HOW MANY TIMES DID MR WINCH RAPE YOU?
4

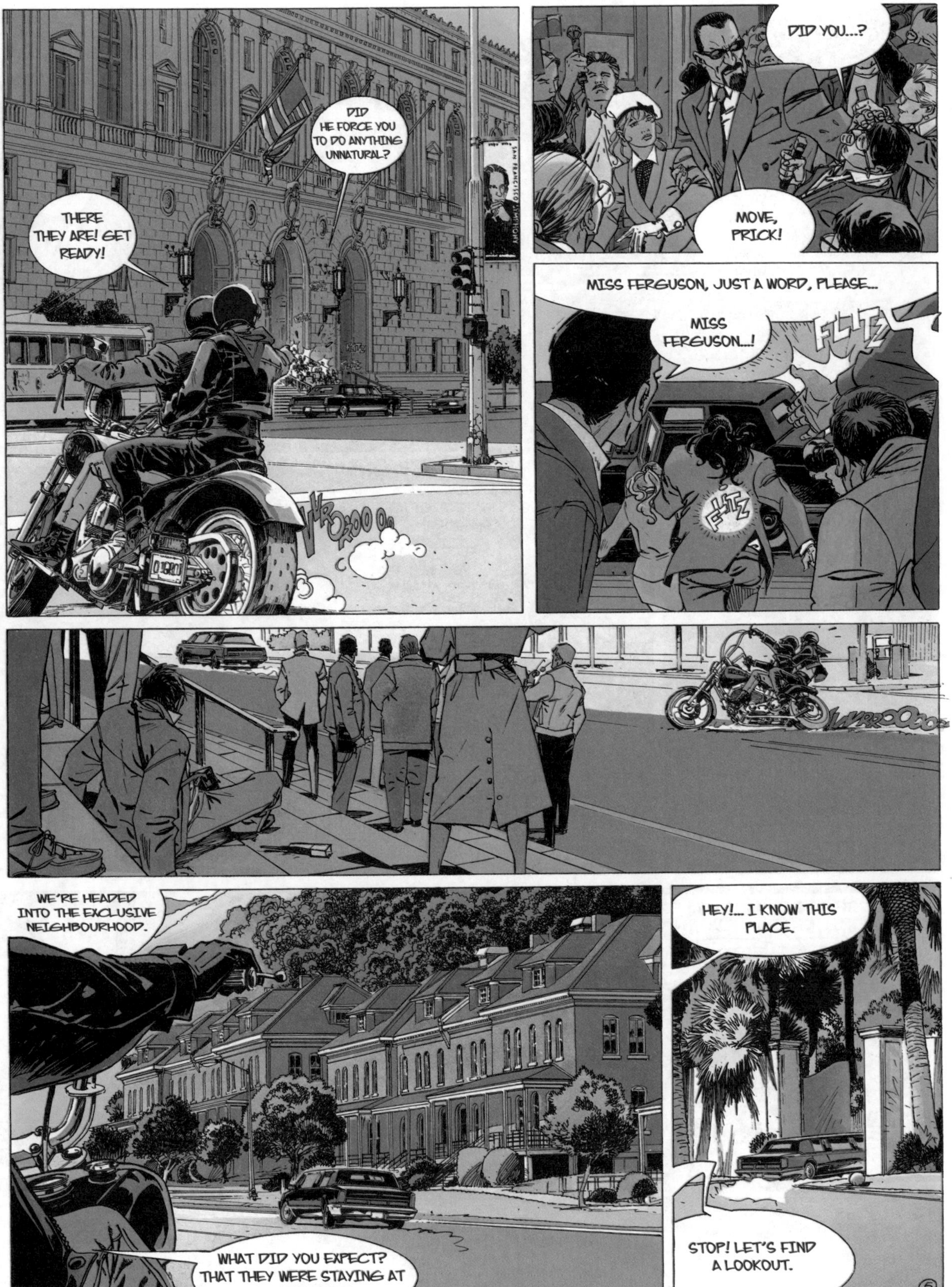
DID HE FORCE YOU TO DO ANYTHING UNNATURAL?
THERE THEY ARE! GET READY!
DID YOU...?
MOVE, PRICK!
MISS FERGUSON, JUST A WORD, PLEASE...
MISS FERGUSON...!
WE'RE HEADED INTO THE EXCLUSIVE NEIGHBOURHOOD.
WHAT DID YOU EXPECT? THAT THEY WERE STAYING AT A CAMPSITE?
HEY!... I KNOW THIS PLACE.
STOP! LET'S FIND A LOOKOUT.

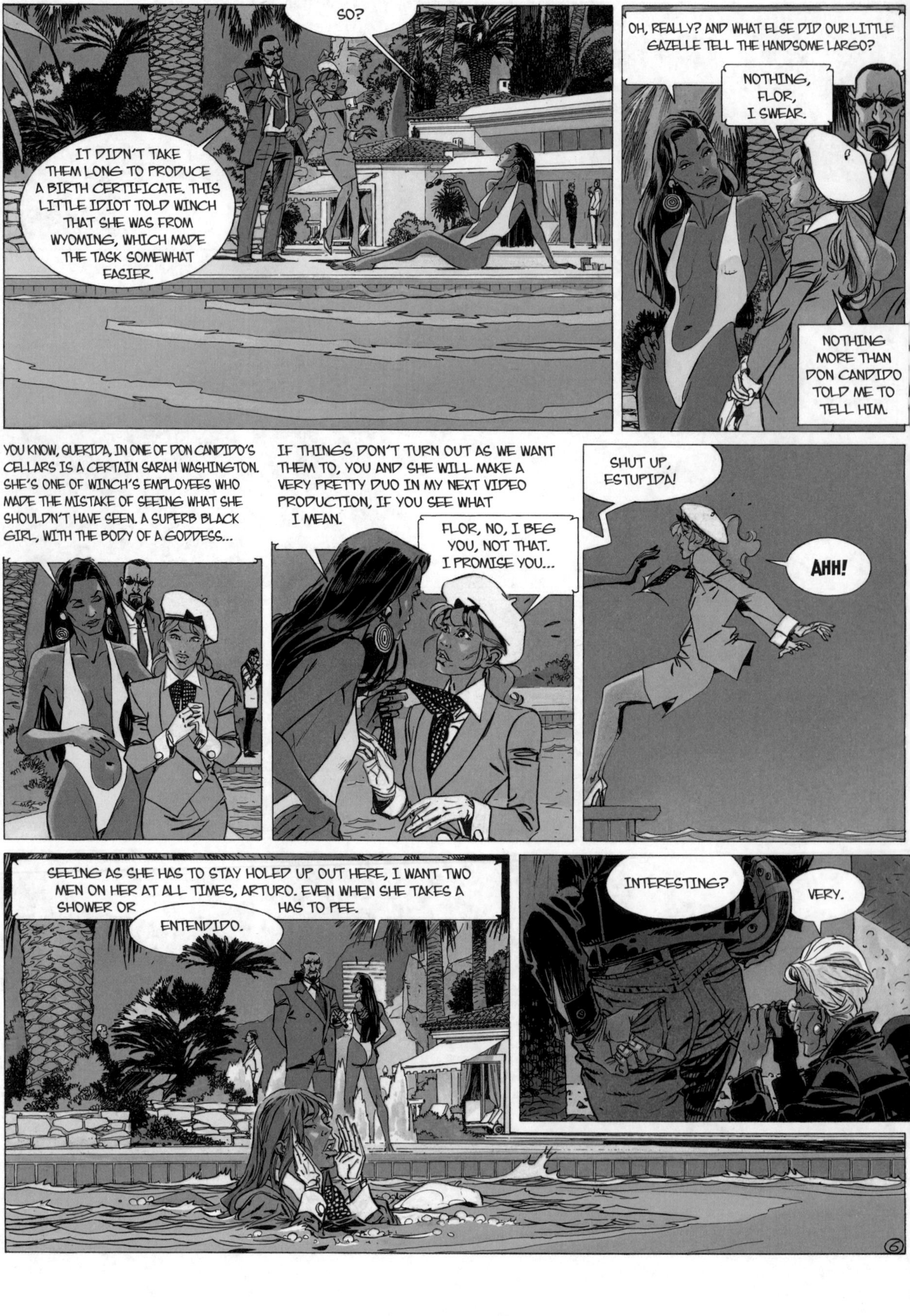
SO?
IT DIDN'T TAKE THEM LONG TO PRODUCE A BIRTH CERTIFICATE. THIS LITTLE IDIOT TOLD WINCH THAT SHE WAS FROM WYOMING, WHICH MADE THE TASK SOMEWHAT EASIER.
OH, REALLY? AND WHAT ELSE DID OUR LITTLE GAZELLE TELL THE HANDSOME LARGO?
NOTHING, FLOR, I SWEAR.
NOTHING MORE THAN DON CANDIDO TOLD ME TO TELL HIM.
YOU KNOW, QUERIDA, IN ONE OF DON CANDIDO'S CELLARS IS A CERTAIN SARAH WASHINGTON. SHE'S ONE OF WINCH'S EMPLOYEES WHO MADE THE MISTAKE OF SEEING WHAT SHE SHOULDN'T HAVE SEEN. A SUPERB BLACK GIRL, WITH THE BODY OF A GODDESS...
IF THINGS DON'T TURN OUT AS WE WANT THEM TO, YOU AND SHE WILL MAKE A VERY PRETTY DUO IN MY NEXT VIDEO PRODUCTION, IF YOU SEE WHAT I MEAN.
FLOR, NO, I BEG YOU, NOT THAT. I PROMISE YOU...
SHUT UP, ESTUPIDA!
AHH!
SEEING AS SHE HAS TO STAY HOLED UP OUT HERE, I WANT TWO MEN ON HER AT ALL TIMES, ARTURO. EVEN WHEN SHE TAKES A SHOWER OR HAS TO PEE.
ENTENDIDO.
INTERESTING?
VERY.
6

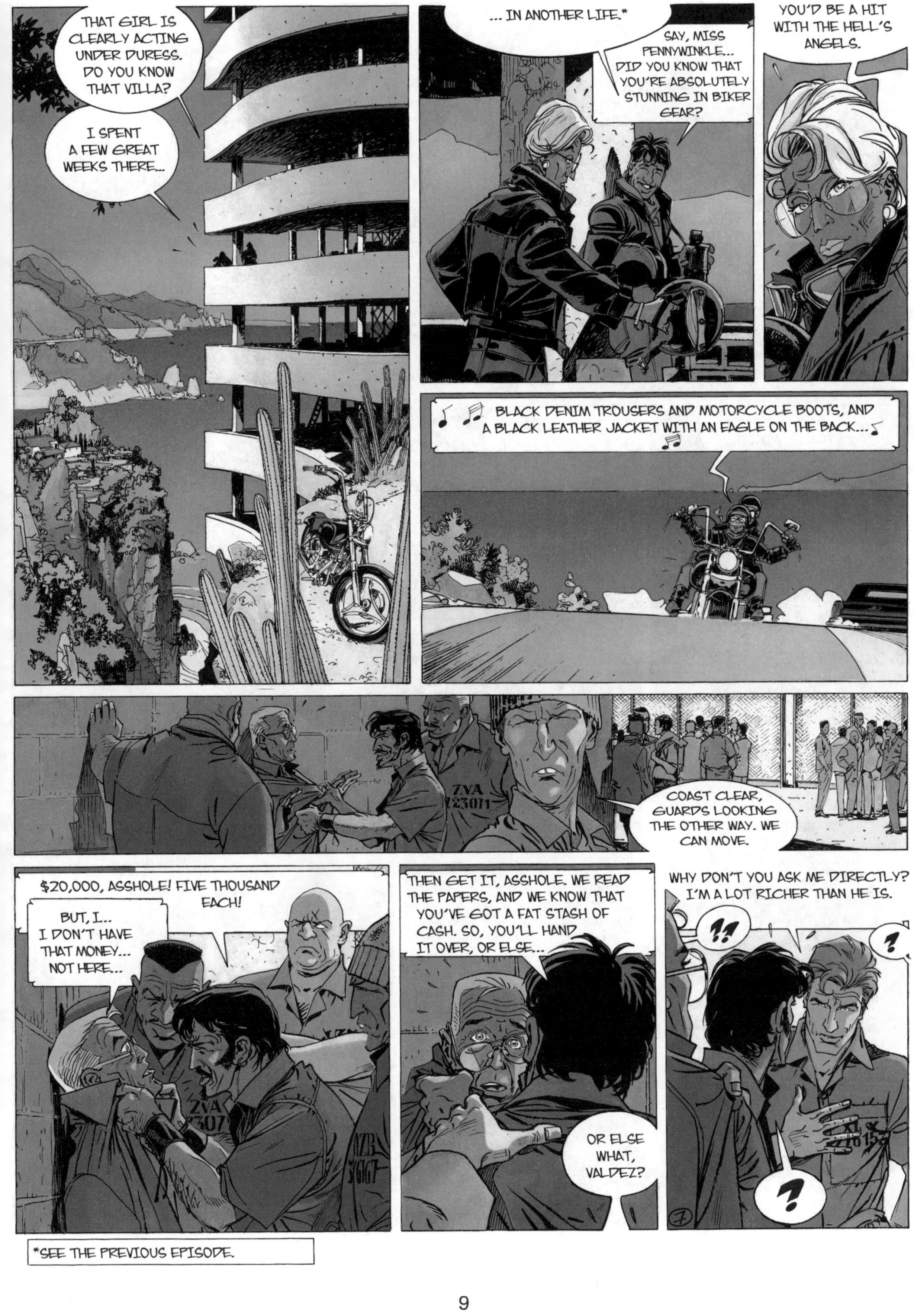
THAT GIRL IS CLEARLY ACTING UNDER DURESS. DO YOU KNOW THAT VILLA?
I SPENT A FEW GREAT WEEKS THERE...
... IN ANOTHER LIFE.*
SAY, MISS PENNYWINKLE... DID YOU KNOW THAT YOU'RE ABSOLUTELY STUNNING IN BIKER GEAR?
YOU'D BE A HIT WITH THE HELL'S ANGELS.
BLACK DENIM TROUSERS AND MOTORCYCLE BOOTS, AND A BLACK LEATHER JACKET WITH AN EAGLE ON THE BACK...
COAST CLEAR, GUARDS LOOKING THE OTHER WAY. WE CAN MOVE.
$20,000, ASSHOLE! FIVE THOUSAND EACH!
BUT, I... I DON'T HAVE THAT MONEY... NOT HERE...
THEN GET IT, ASSHOLE. WE READ THE PAPERS, AND WE KNOW THAT YOU'VE GOT A FAT STASH OF CASH. SO, YOU'LL HAND IT OVER, OR ELSE...
OR ELSE WHAT, VALDEZ?
WHY DON'T YOU ASK ME DIRECTLY? I'M A LOT RICHER THAN HE IS.
?!
?
?

*SEE THE PREVIOUS EPISODE.

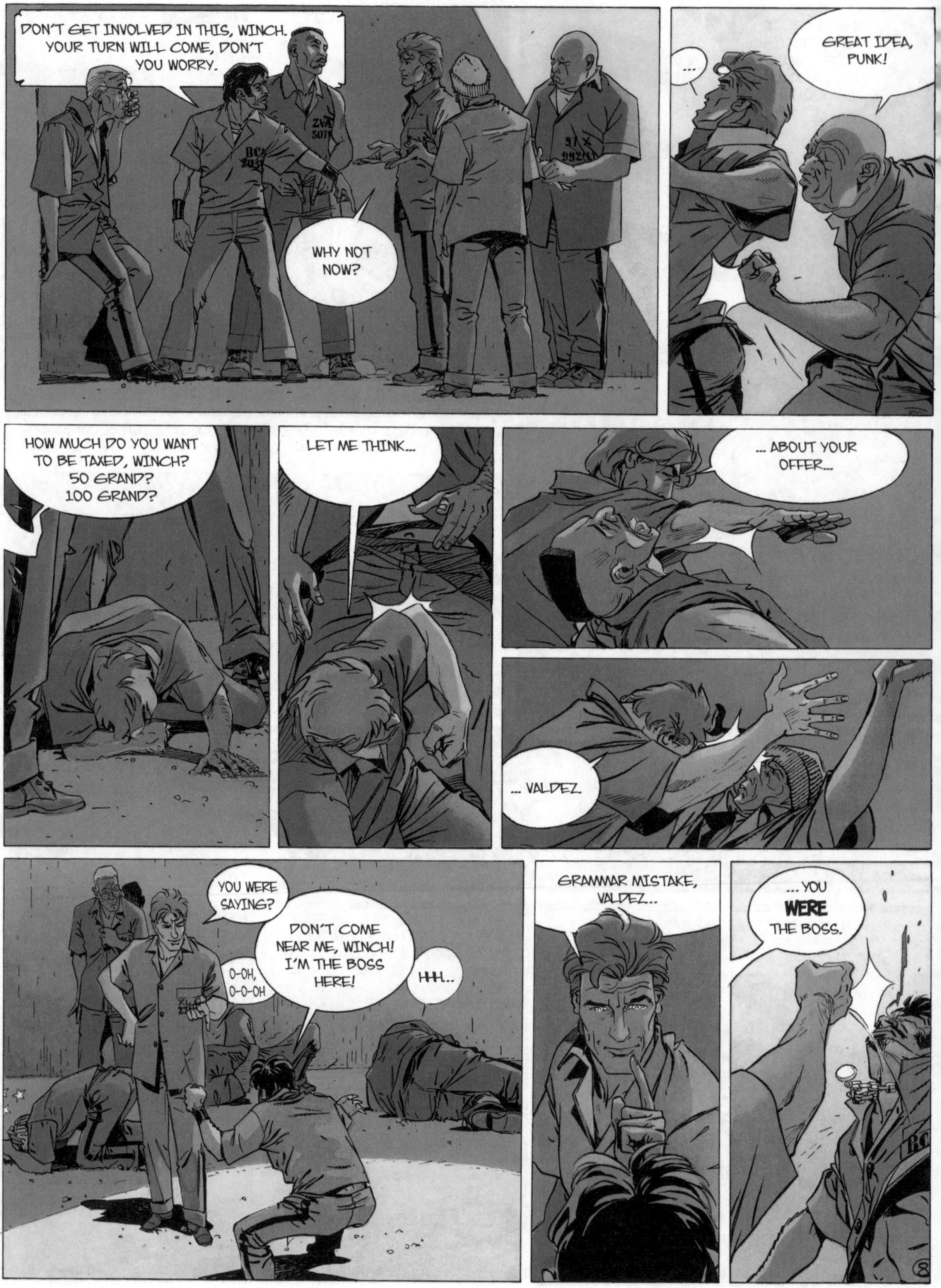
DON'T GET INVOLVED IN THIS, WINCH. YOUR TURN WILL COME, DON'T YOU WORRY.
WHY NOT NOW?
...
GREAT IDEA, PUNK!
HOW MUCH DO YOU WANT TO BE TAXED, WINCH? 50 GRAND? 100 GRAND?
LET ME THINK...
... ABOUT YOUR OFFER...
... VALDEZ.
YOU WERE SAYING?
DON'T COME NEAR ME, WINCH! I'M THE BOSS HERE!
O-OH, O-O-OH
HHH...
GRAMMAR MISTAKE, VALDEZ...
... YOU WERE THE BOSS.

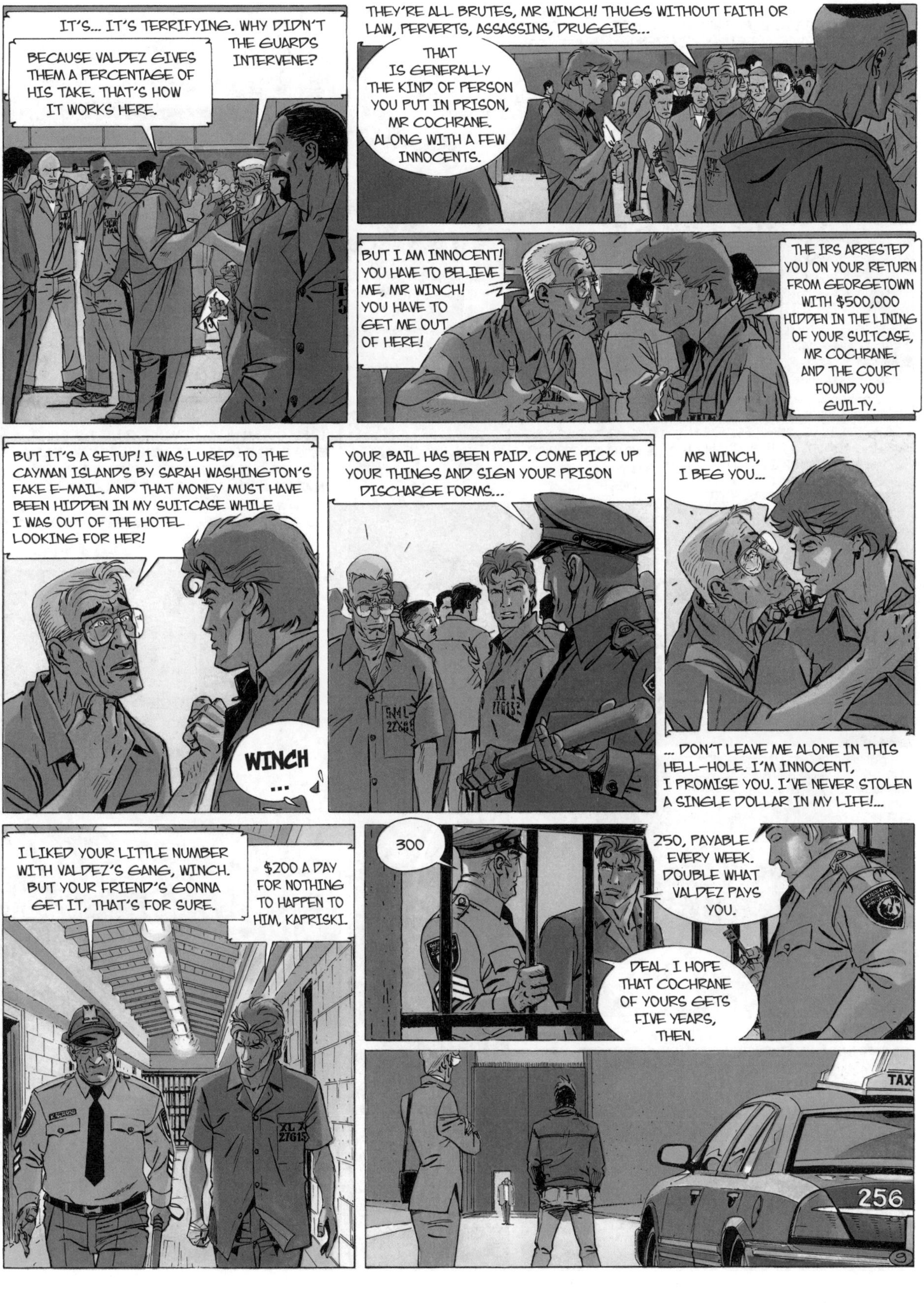
IT'S... IT'S TERRIFYING. WHY DIDN'T THE GUARDS INTERVENE?
BECAUSE VALDEZ GIVES THEM A PERCENTAGE OF HIS TAKE. THAT'S HOW IT WORKS HERE.
THEY'RE ALL BRUTES, MR WINCH! THUGS WITHOUT FAITH OR LAW, PERVERTS, ASSASSINS, DRUGGIES...
THAT IS GENERALLY THE KIND OF PERSON YOU PUT IN PRISON, MR COCHRANE. ALONG WITH A FEW INNOCENTS.
BUT I AM INNOCENT! YOU HAVE TO BELIEVE ME, MR WINCH! YOU HAVE TO GET ME OUT OF HERE!
THE IRS ARRESTED YOU ON YOUR RETURN FROM GEORGETOWN WITH $500,000 HIDDEN IN THE LINING OF YOUR SUITCASE, MR COCHRANE. AND THE COURT FOUND YOU GUILTY.
BUT IT'S A SETUP! I WAS LURED TO THE CAYMAN ISLANDS BY SARAH WASHINGTON'S FAKE E-MAIL. AND THAT MONEY MUST HAVE BEEN HIDDEN IN MY SUITCASE WHILE I WAS OUT OF THE HOTEL LOOKING FOR HER!
WINCH ...
YOUR BAIL HAS BEEN PAID. COME PICK UP YOUR THINGS AND SIGN YOUR PRISON DISCHARGE FORMS...
MR WINCH, I BEG YOU...
... DON'T LEAVE ME ALONE IN THIS HELL-HOLE. I'M INNOCENT, I PROMISE YOU. I'VE NEVER STOLEN A SINGLE DOLLAR IN MY LIFE!...
I LIKED YOUR LITTLE NUMBER WITH VALDEZ'S GANG, WINCH. BUT YOUR FRIEND'S GONNA GET IT, THAT'S FOR SURE.
$200 A DAY FOR NOTHING TO HAPPEN TO HIM, KAPRISKI.
300
250, PAYABLE EVERY WEEK. DOUBLE WHAT VALDEZ PAYS YOU.
DEAL. I HOPE THAT COCHRANE OF YOURS GETS FIVE YEARS, THEN.
TAXI
256

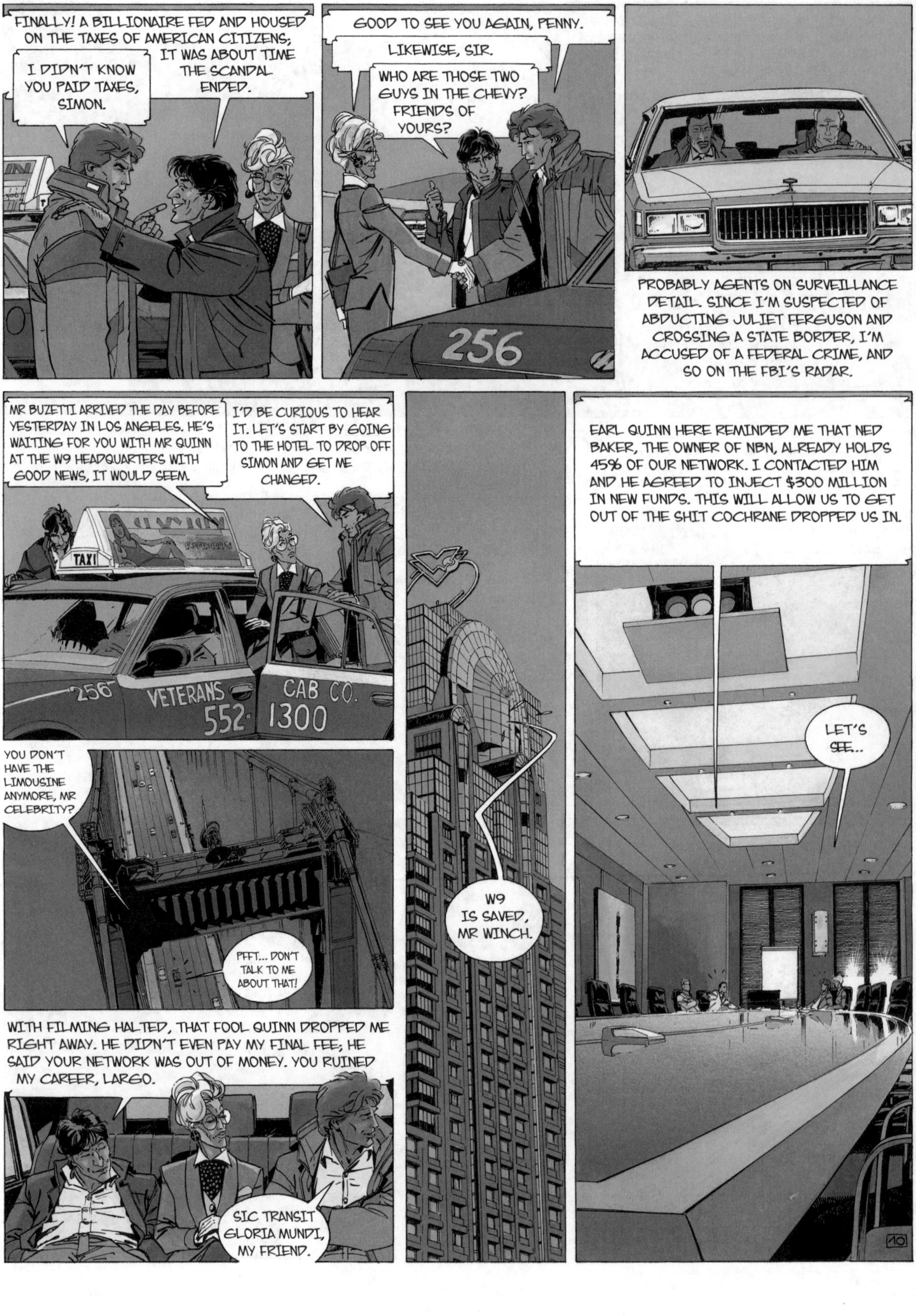
FINALLY! A BILLIONAIRE FED AND HOUSED ON THE TAXES OF AMERICAN CITIZENS; IT WAS ABOUT TIME THE SCANDAL ENDED.
I DIDN'T KNOW YOU PAID TAXES, SIMON.
GOOD TO SEE YOU AGAIN, PENNY.
LIKEWISE, SIR.
WHO ARE THOSE TWO GUYS IN THE CHEVY? FRIENDS OF YOURS?
256
PROBABLY AGENTS ON SURVEILLANCE DETAIL. SINCE I'M SUSPECTED OF ABDUCTING JULIET FERGUSON AND CROSSING A STATE BORDER, I'M ACCUSED OF A FEDERAL CRIME, AND SO ON THE FBI'S RADAR.
MR BUZETTI ARRIVED THE DAY BEFORE YESTERDAY IN LOS ANGELES. HE'S WAITING FOR YOU WITH MR QUINN AT THE W9 HEADQUARTERS WITH GOOD NEWS, IT WOULD SEEM.
I'D BE CURIOUS TO HEAR IT. LET'S START BY GOING TO THE HOTEL TO DROP OFF SIMON AND GET ME CHANGED.
TAXI
256 VETERANS CAB CO. 552-1300
YOU DON'T HAVE THE LIMOUSINE ANYMORE, MR CELEBRITY?
PFFT... DON'T TALK TO ME ABOUT THAT!
WITH FILMING HALTED, THAT FOOL QUINN DROPPED ME RIGHT AWAY. HE DIDN'T EVEN PAY MY FINAL FEE; HE SAID YOUR NETWORK WAS OUT OF MONEY. YOU RUINED MY CAREER, LARGO.
SIC TRANSIT GLORIA MUNDI, MY FRIEND.
W9 IS SAVED, MR WINCH.
EARL QUINN HERE REMINDED ME THAT NED BAKER, THE OWNER OF NBN, ALREADY HOLDS 45% OF OUR NETWORK. I CONTACTED HIM AND HE AGREED TO INJECT $300 MILLION IN NEW FUNDS. THIS WILL ALLOW US TO GET OUT OF THE SHIT COCHRANE DROPPED US IN.
LET'S SEE...
10

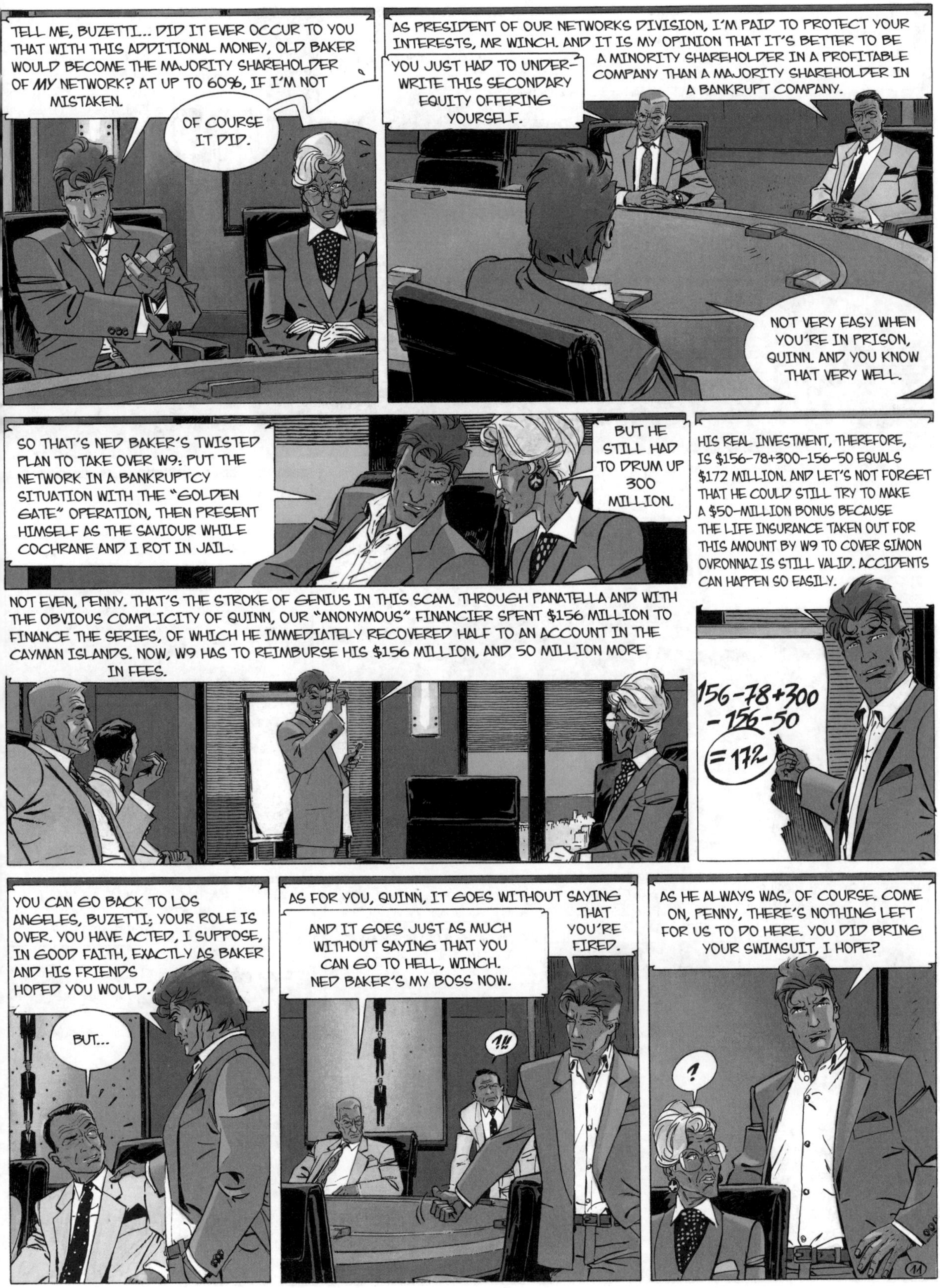
TELL ME, BUZETTI... DID IT EVER OCCUR TO YOU THAT WITH THIS ADDITIONAL MONEY, OLD BAKER WOULD BECOME THE MAJORITY SHAREHOLDER OF MY NETWORK? AT UP TO 60%, IF I'M NOT MISTAKEN.
OF COURSE IT DID.
AS PRESIDENT OF OUR NETWORKS DIVISION, I'M PAID TO PROTECT YOUR INTERESTS, MR WINCH. AND IT IS MY OPINION THAT IT'S BETTER TO BE A MINORITY SHAREHOLDER IN A PROFITABLE COMPANY THAN A MAJORITY SHAREHOLDER IN A BANKRUPT COMPANY.
YOU JUST HAD TO UNDERWRITE THIS SECONDARY EQUITY OFFERING YOURSELF.
NOT VERY EASY WHEN YOU'RE IN PRISON, QUINN. AND YOU KNOW THAT VERY WELL.
SO THAT'S NED BAKER'S TWISTED PLAN TO TAKE OVER W9: PUT THE NETWORK IN A BANKRUPTCY SITUATION WITH THE "GOLDEN GATE" OPERATION, THEN PRESENT HIMSELF AS THE SAVIOUR WHILE COCHRANE AND I ROT IN JAIL.
BUT HE STILL HAD TO DRUM UP 300 MILLION.
NOT EVEN, PENNY. THAT'S THE STROKE OF GENIUS IN THIS SCAM. THROUGH PANATELLA AND WITH THE OBVIOUS COMPLICITY OF QUINN, OUR "ANONYMOUS" FINANCIER SPENT $156 MILLION TO FINANCE THE SERIES, OF WHICH HE IMMEDIATELY RECOVERED HALF TO AN ACCOUNT IN THE CAYMAN ISLANDS. NOW, W9 HAS TO REIMBURSE HIS $156 MILLION, AND 50 MILLION MORE IN FEES.
HIS REAL INVESTMENT, THEREFORE, IS $156–78+300–156–50 EQUALS $172 MILLION. AND LET'S NOT FORGET THAT HE COULD STILL TRY TO MAKE A $50-MILLION BONUS BECAUSE THE LIFE INSURANCE TAKEN OUT FOR THIS AMOUNT BY W9 TO COVER SIMON OVRONNAZ IS STILL VALID. ACCIDENTS CAN HAPPEN SO EASILY.
156–78+300
–156–50
=172
YOU CAN GO BACK TO LOS ANGELES, BUZETTI; YOUR ROLE IS OVER. YOU HAVE ACTED, I SUPPOSE, IN GOOD FAITH, EXACTLY AS BAKER AND HIS FRIENDS HOPED YOU WOULD.
BUT...
AS FOR YOU, QUINN, IT GOES WITHOUT SAYING THAT YOU'RE FIRED.
AND IT GOES JUST AS MUCH WITHOUT SAYING THAT YOU CAN GO TO HELL, WINCH. NED BAKER'S MY BOSS NOW.
!!!
AS HE ALWAYS WAS, OF COURSE. COME ON, PENNY, THERE'S NOTHING LEFT FOR US TO DO HERE. YOU DID BRING YOUR SWIMSUIT, I HOPE?
?
11

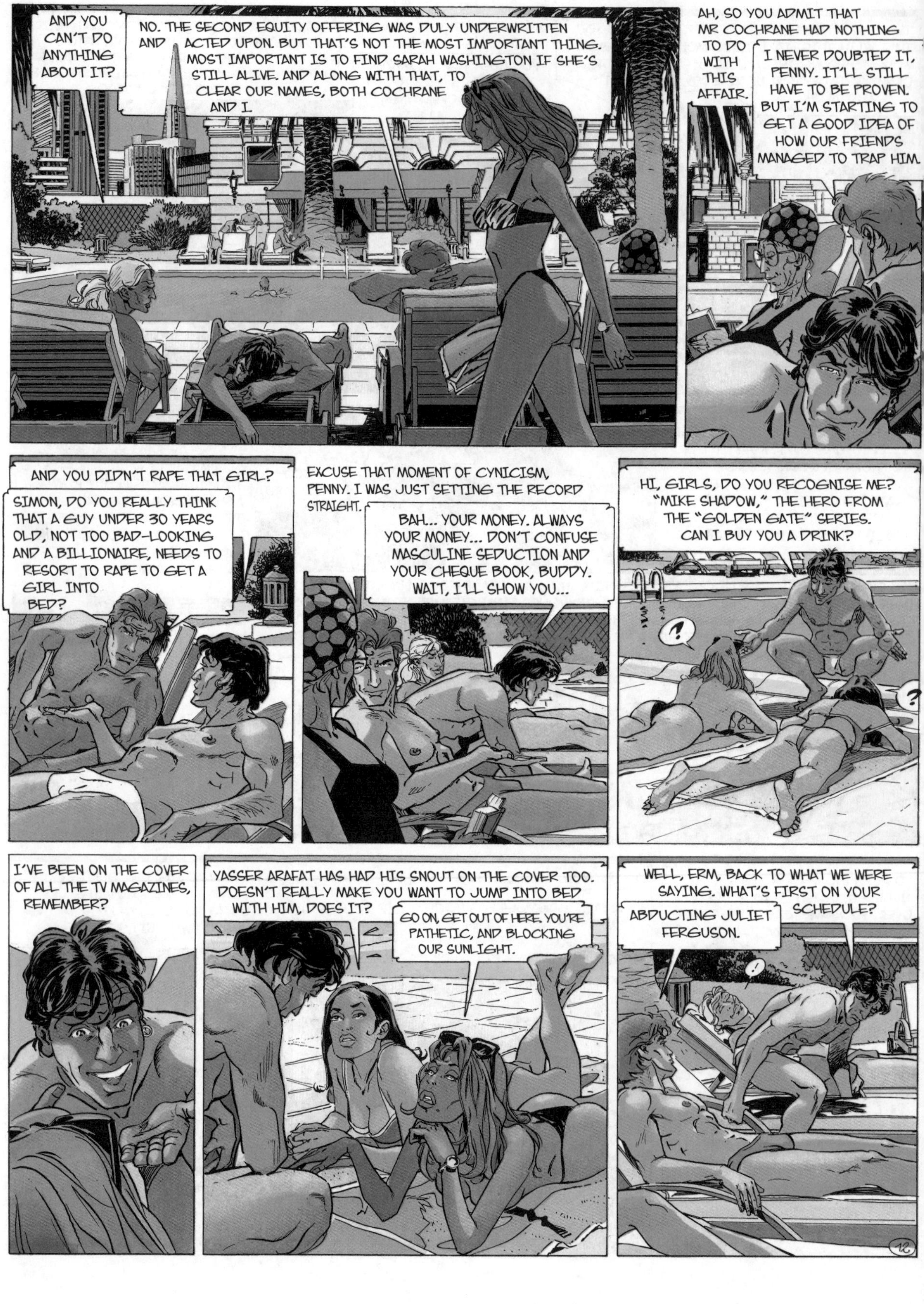
AND YOU CAN'T DO ANYTHING ABOUT IT?
NO. THE SECOND EQUITY OFFERING WAS DULY UNDERWRITTEN AND ACTED UPON. BUT THAT'S NOT THE MOST IMPORTANT THING. MOST IMPORTANT IS TO FIND SARAH WASHINGTON IF SHE'S STILL ALIVE. AND ALONG WITH THAT, TO CLEAR OUR NAMES, BOTH COCHRANE AND I.
AH, SO YOU ADMIT THAT MR COCHRANE HAD NOTHING TO DO WITH THIS AFFAIR.
I NEVER DOUBTED IT, PENNY. IT'LL STILL HAVE TO BE PROVEN. BUT I'M STARTING TO GET A GOOD IDEA OF HOW OUR FRIENDS MANAGED TO TRAP HIM.
AND YOU DIDN'T RAPE THAT GIRL?
SIMON, DO YOU REALLY THINK THAT A GUY UNDER 30 YEARS OLD, NOT TOO BAD-LOOKING AND A BILLIONAIRE, NEEDS TO RESORT TO RAPE TO GET A GIRL INTO BED?
EXCUSE THAT MOMENT OF CYNICISM, PENNY. I WAS JUST SETTING THE RECORD STRAIGHT.
BAH... YOUR MONEY. ALWAYS YOUR MONEY... DON'T CONFUSE MASCULINE SEDUCTION AND YOUR CHEQUE BOOK, BUDDY. WAIT, I'LL SHOW YOU...
HI, GIRLS, DO YOU RECOGNISE ME? "MIKE SHADOW," THE HERO FROM THE "GOLDEN GATE" SERIES. CAN I BUY YOU A DRINK?
?
?
I'VE BEEN ON THE COVER OF ALL THE TV MAGAZINES, REMEMBER?
YASSER ARAFAT HAS HAD HIS SNOUT ON THE COVER TOO. DOESN'T REALLY MAKE YOU WANT TO JUMP INTO BED WITH HIM, DOES IT?
GO ON, GET OUT OF HERE. YOU'RE PATHETIC, AND BLOCKING OUR SUNLIGHT.
WELL, ERM, BACK TO WHAT WE WERE SAYING. WHAT'S FIRST ON YOUR SCHEDULE?
ABDUCTING JULIET FERGUSON.
!
12

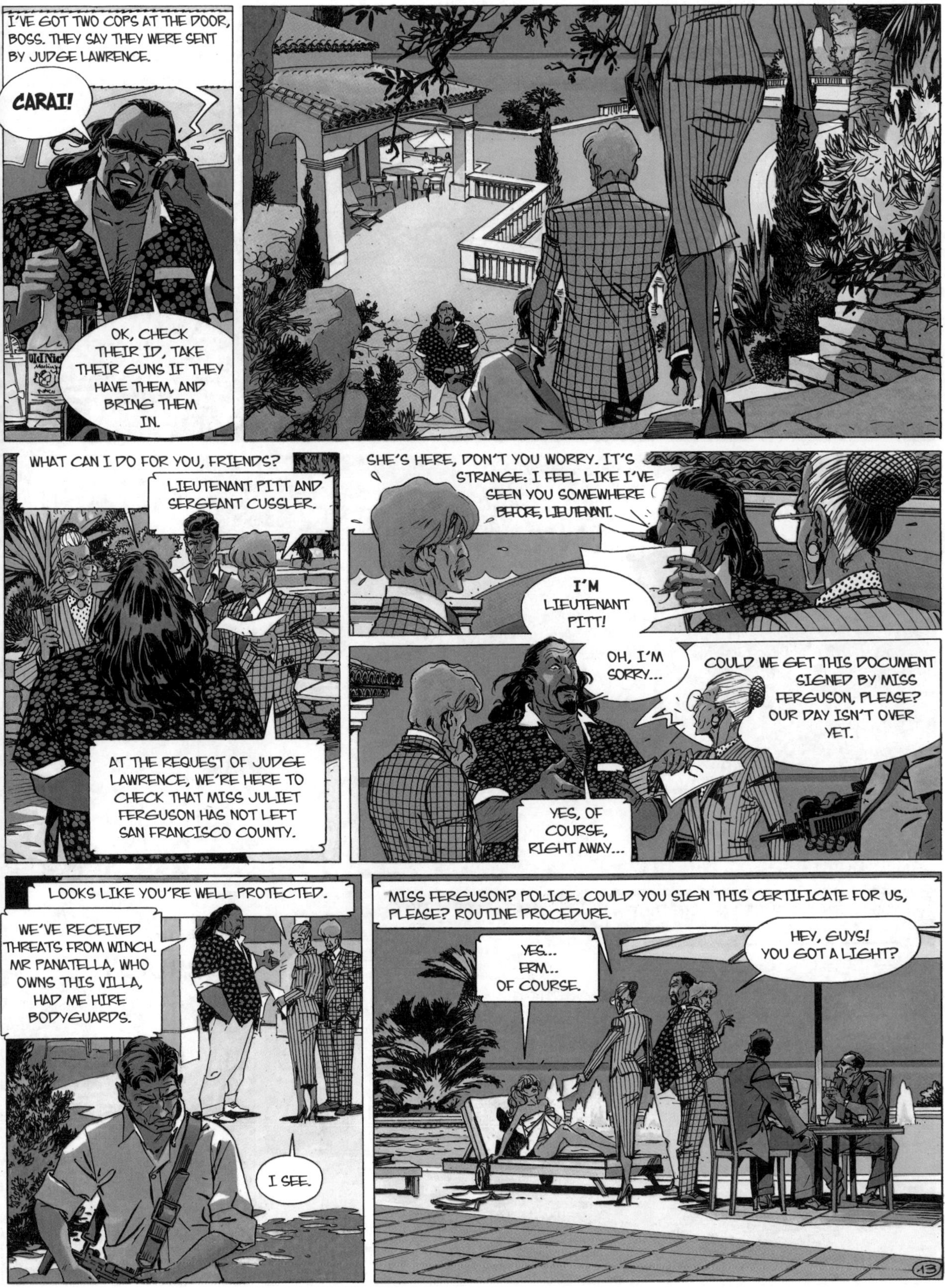
I'VE GOT TWO COPS AT THE DOOR, BOSS. THEY SAY THEY WERE SENT BY JUDGE LAWRENCE.
CARAI!
OK, CHECK THEIR ID, TAKE THEIR GUNS IF THEY HAVE THEM, AND BRING THEM IN.
WHAT CAN I DO FOR YOU, FRIENDS?
LIEUTENANT PITT AND SERGEANT CUSSLER.
AT THE REQUEST OF JUDGE LAWRENCE, WE'RE HERE TO CHECK THAT MISS JULIET FERGUSON HAS NOT LEFT SAN FRANCISCO COUNTY.
SHE'S HERE, DON'T YOU WORRY. IT'S STRANGE: I FEEL LIKE I'VE SEEN YOU SOMEWHERE BEFORE, LIEUTENANT.
I'M LIEUTENANT PITT!
OH, I'M SORRY...
COULD WE GET THIS DOCUMENT SIGNED BY MISS FERGUSON, PLEASE? OUR DAY ISN'T OVER YET.
YES, OF COURSE, RIGHT AWAY...
LOOKS LIKE YOU'RE WELL PROTECTED.
WE'VE RECEIVED THREATS FROM WINCH. MR PANATELLA, WHO OWNS THIS VILLA, HAD ME HIRE BODYGUARDS.
I SEE.
MISS FERGUSON? POLICE. COULD YOU SIGN THIS CERTIFICATE FOR US, PLEASE? ROUTINE PROCEDURE.
YES... ERM... OF COURSE.
HEY, GUYS! YOU GOT A LIGHT?
13

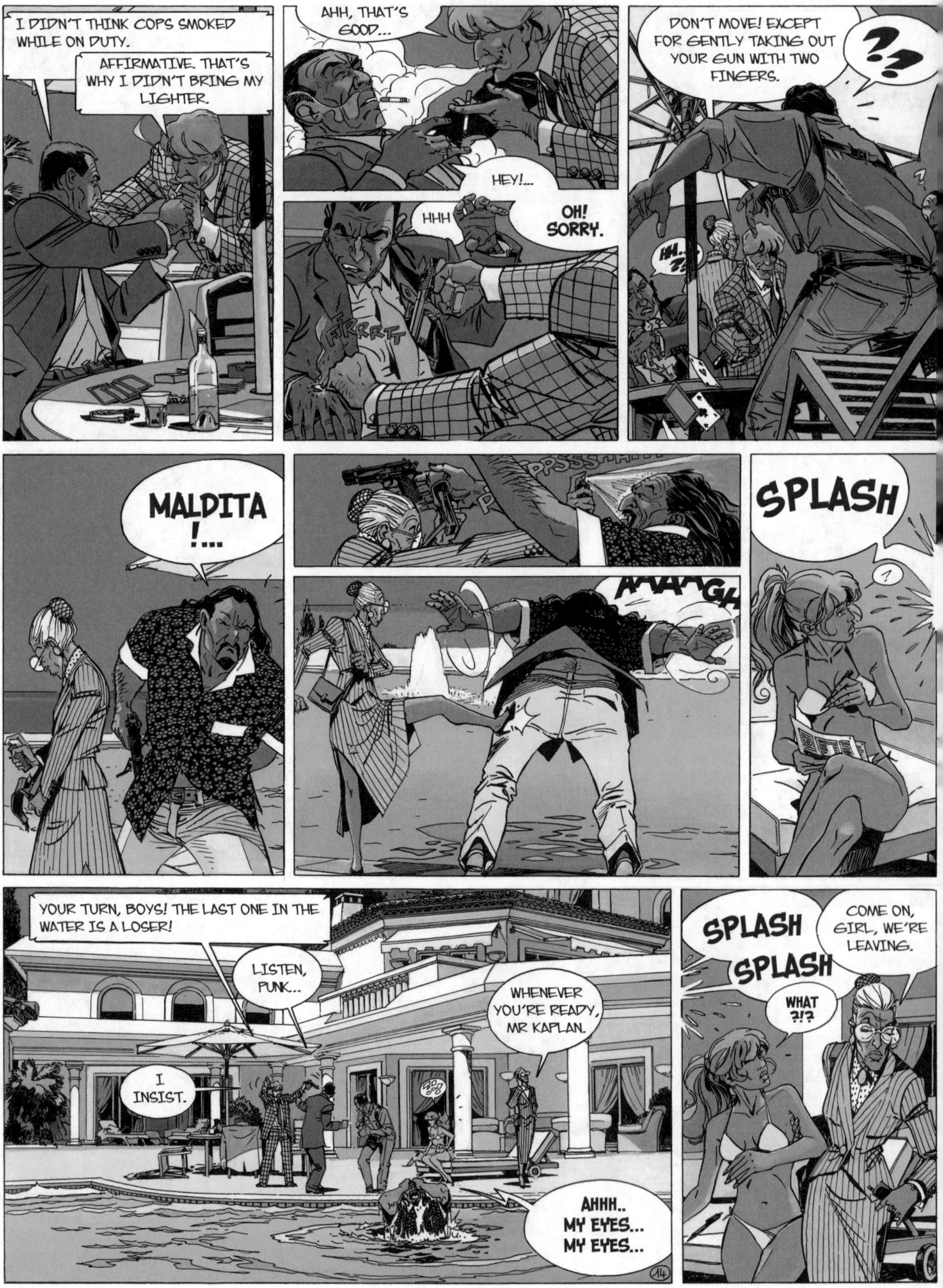
I DIDN'T THINK COPS SMOKED WHILE ON DUTY.
AFFIRMATIVE. THAT'S WHY I DIDN'T BRING MY LIGHTER.
AHH, THAT'S GOOD...
HEY!...
HHH
OH! SORRY.
FRRRTT
DON'T MOVE! EXCEPT FOR GENTLY TAKING OUT YOUR GUN WITH TWO FINGERS.
??
HH..??
MALDITA !...
SPLASH
AAAAGH
?
YOUR TURN, BOYS! THE LAST ONE IN THE WATER IS A LOSER!
LISTEN, PUNK...
WHENEVER YOU'RE READY, MR KAPLAN.
I INSIST.
AHHH.. MY EYES... MY EYES...
SPLASH
SPLASH
COME ON, GIRL, WE'RE LEAVING.
WHAT ?!?
14

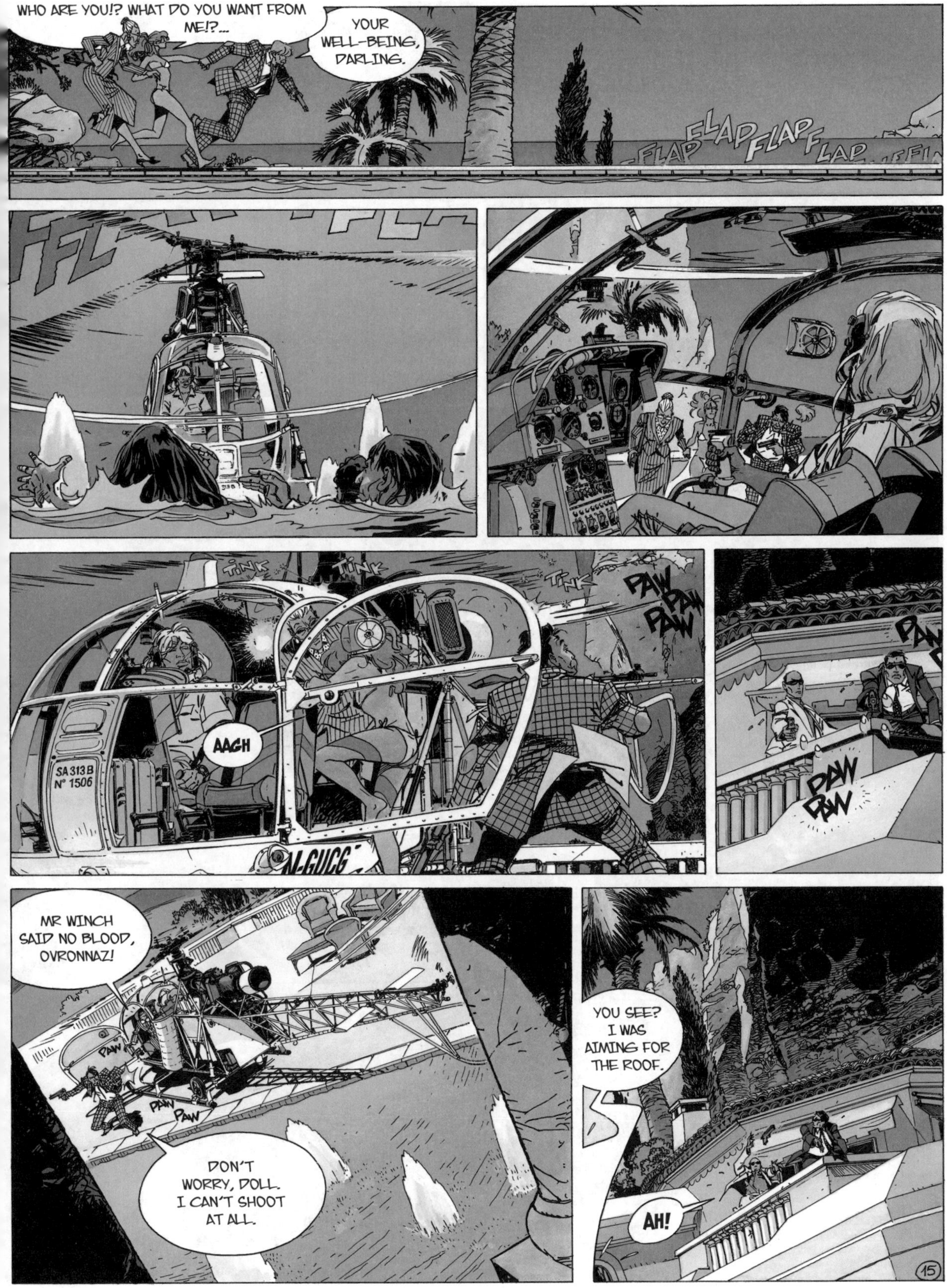

WHO ARE YOU!? WHAT DO YOU WANT FROM ME!?...
YOUR WELL-BEING, DARLING.
FLAP FLAP FLAP FLAP
TINK
TINK
TINK
PAW PAW PAW
AAGH
SA 313 B N° 1506
PAW PAW
PAW PAW
MR WINCH SAID NO BLOOD, OVRONNAZ!
PAW
PAW PAW
DON'T WORRY, DOLL. I CAN'T SHOOT AT ALL.
YOU SEE? I WAS AIMING FOR THE ROOF.
AH!
15

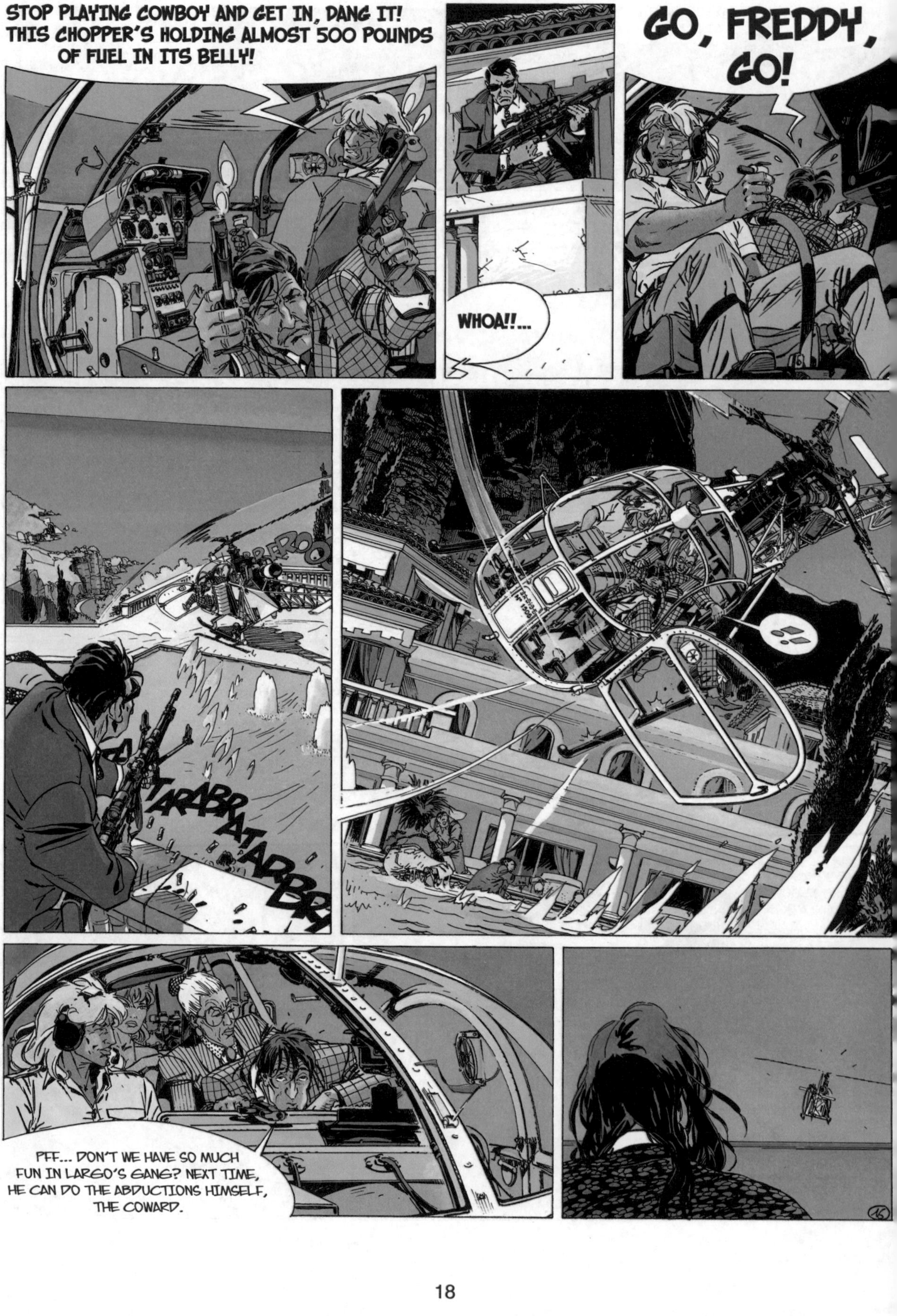
STOP PLAYING COWBOY AND GET IN, DANG IT! THIS CHOPPER'S HOLDING ALMOST 500 POUNDS OF FUEL IN ITS BELLY!
GO, FREDDY, GO!
WHOA!!...
PFF... DON'T WE HAVE SO MUCH FUN IN LARGO'S GANG? NEXT TIME, HE CAN DO THE ABDUCTIONS HIMSELF, THE COWARD.

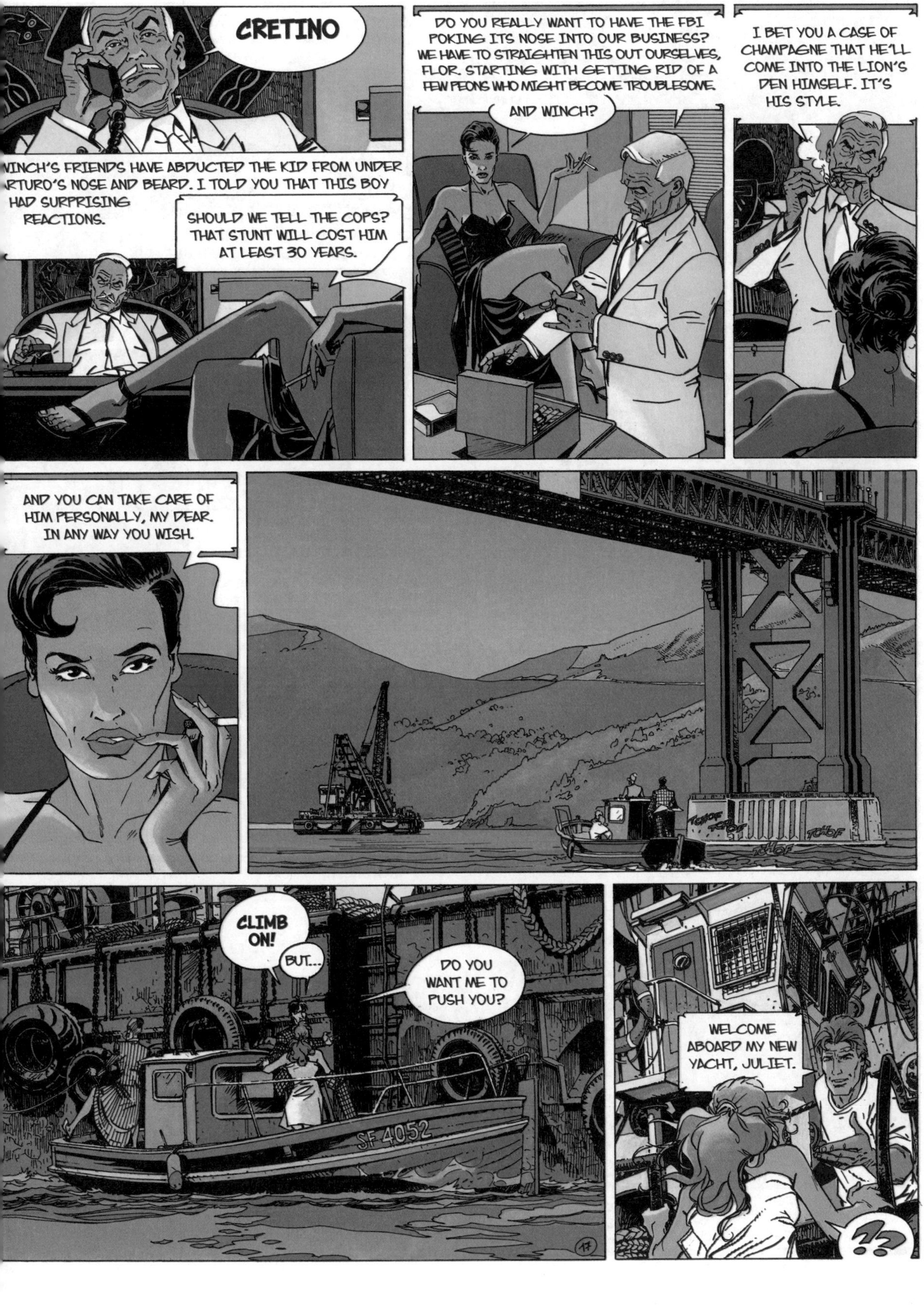
CRETINO
WINCH'S FRIENDS HAVE ABDUCTED THE KID FROM UNDER ARTURO'S NOSE AND BEARD. I TOLD YOU THAT THIS BOY HAD SURPRISING REACTIONS.
SHOULD WE TELL THE COPS? THAT STUNT WILL COST HIM AT LEAST 30 YEARS.
DO YOU REALLY WANT TO HAVE THE FBI POKING ITS NOSE INTO OUR BUSINESS? WE HAVE TO STRAIGHTEN THIS OUT OURSELVES, FLOR. STARTING WITH GETTING RID OF A FEW PEONS WHO MIGHT BECOME TROUBLESOME.
AND WINCH?
I BET YOU A CASE OF CHAMPAGNE THAT HE'LL COME INTO THE LION'S DEN HIMSELF. IT'S HIS STYLE.
AND YOU CAN TAKE CARE OF HIM PERSONALLY, MY DEAR. IN ANY WAY YOU WISH.
TCHOF
TCHOF
TCHOF
TCHOF
TCHOF
CLIMB ON!
BUT...
DO YOU WANT ME TO PUSH YOU?
SF 4052
17
WELCOME ABOARD MY NEW YACHT, JULIET.
?!?

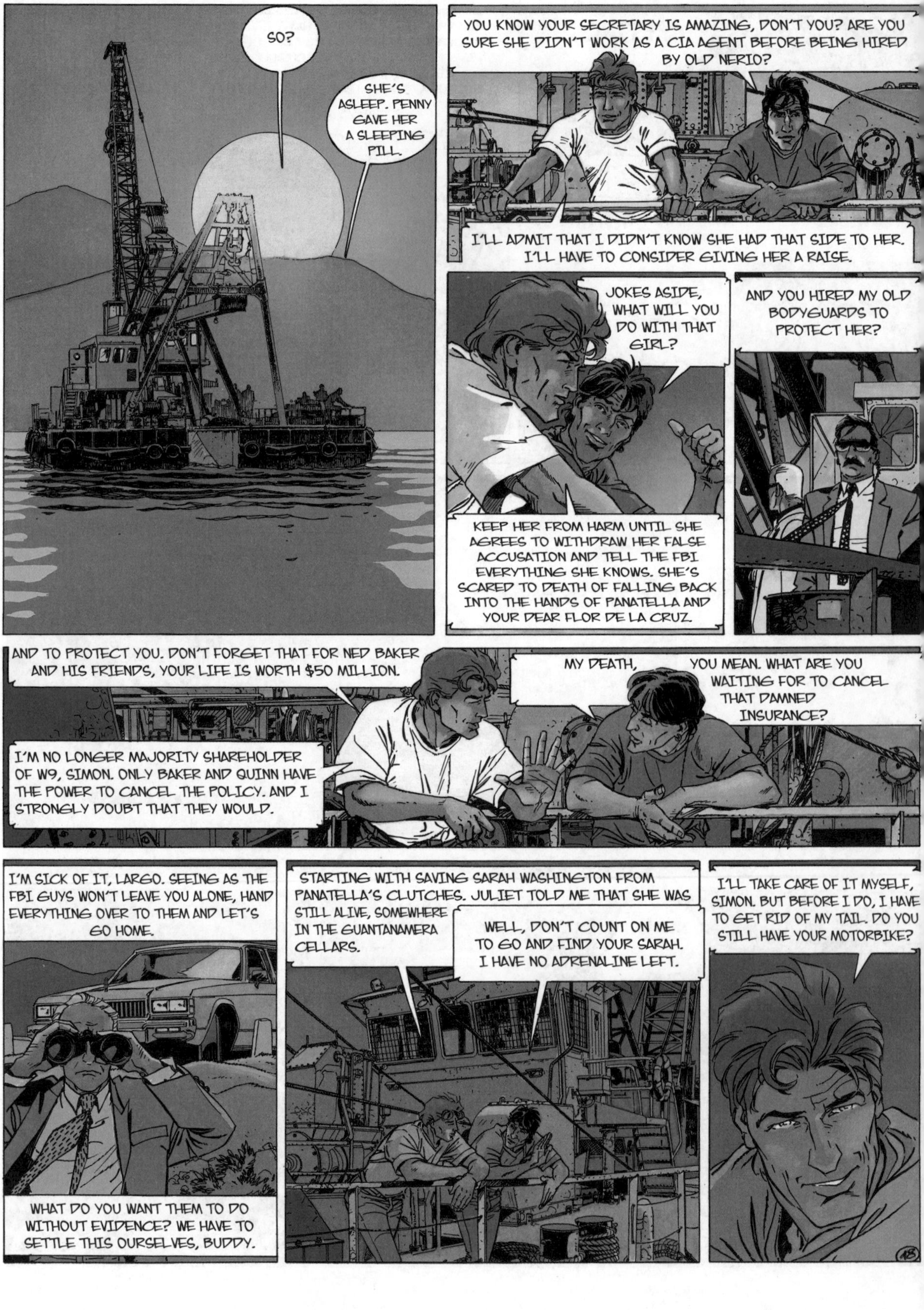

SO?
SHE'S ASLEEP. PENNY GAVE HER A SLEEPING PILL.
YOU KNOW YOUR SECRETARY IS AMAZING, DON'T YOU? ARE YOU SURE SHE DIDN'T WORK AS A CIA AGENT BEFORE BEING HIRED BY OLD NERIO?
I'LL ADMIT THAT I DIDN'T KNOW SHE HAD THAT SIDE TO HER. I'LL HAVE TO CONSIDER GIVING HER A RAISE.
JOKES ASIDE, WHAT WILL YOU DO WITH THAT GIRL?
KEEP HER FROM HARM UNTIL SHE AGREES TO WITHDRAW HER FALSE ACCUSATION AND TELL THE FBI EVERYTHING SHE KNOWS. SHE'S SCARED TO DEATH OF FALLING BACK INTO THE HANDS OF PANATELLA AND YOUR DEAR FLOR DE LA CRUZ.
AND YOU HIRED MY OLD BODYGUARDS TO PROTECT HER?
AND TO PROTECT YOU. DON'T FORGET THAT FOR NED BAKER AND HIS FRIENDS, YOUR LIFE IS WORTH $50 MILLION.
MY DEATH,
YOU MEAN. WHAT ARE YOU WAITING FOR TO CANCEL THAT DAMNED INSURANCE?
I'M NO LONGER MAJORITY SHAREHOLDER OF W9, SIMON. ONLY BAKER AND QUINN HAVE THE POWER TO CANCEL THE POLICY. AND I STRONGLY DOUBT THAT THEY WOULD.
I'M SICK OF IT, LARGO. SEEING AS THE FBI GUYS WON'T LEAVE YOU ALONE, HAND EVERYTHING OVER TO THEM AND LET'S GO HOME.
WHAT DO YOU WANT THEM TO DO WITHOUT EVIDENCE? WE HAVE TO SETTLE THIS OURSELVES, BUDDY.
STARTING WITH SAVING SARAH WASHINGTON FROM PANATELLA'S CLUTCHES. JULIET TOLD ME THAT SHE WAS STILL ALIVE, SOMEWHERE IN THE GUANTANAMERA CELLARS.
WELL, DON'T COUNT ON ME TO GO AND FIND YOUR SARAH. I HAVE NO ADRENALINE LEFT.
I'LL TAKE CARE OF IT MYSELF, SIMON. BUT BEFORE I DO, I HAVE TO GET RID OF MY TAIL. DO YOU STILL HAVE YOUR MOTORBIKE?
18

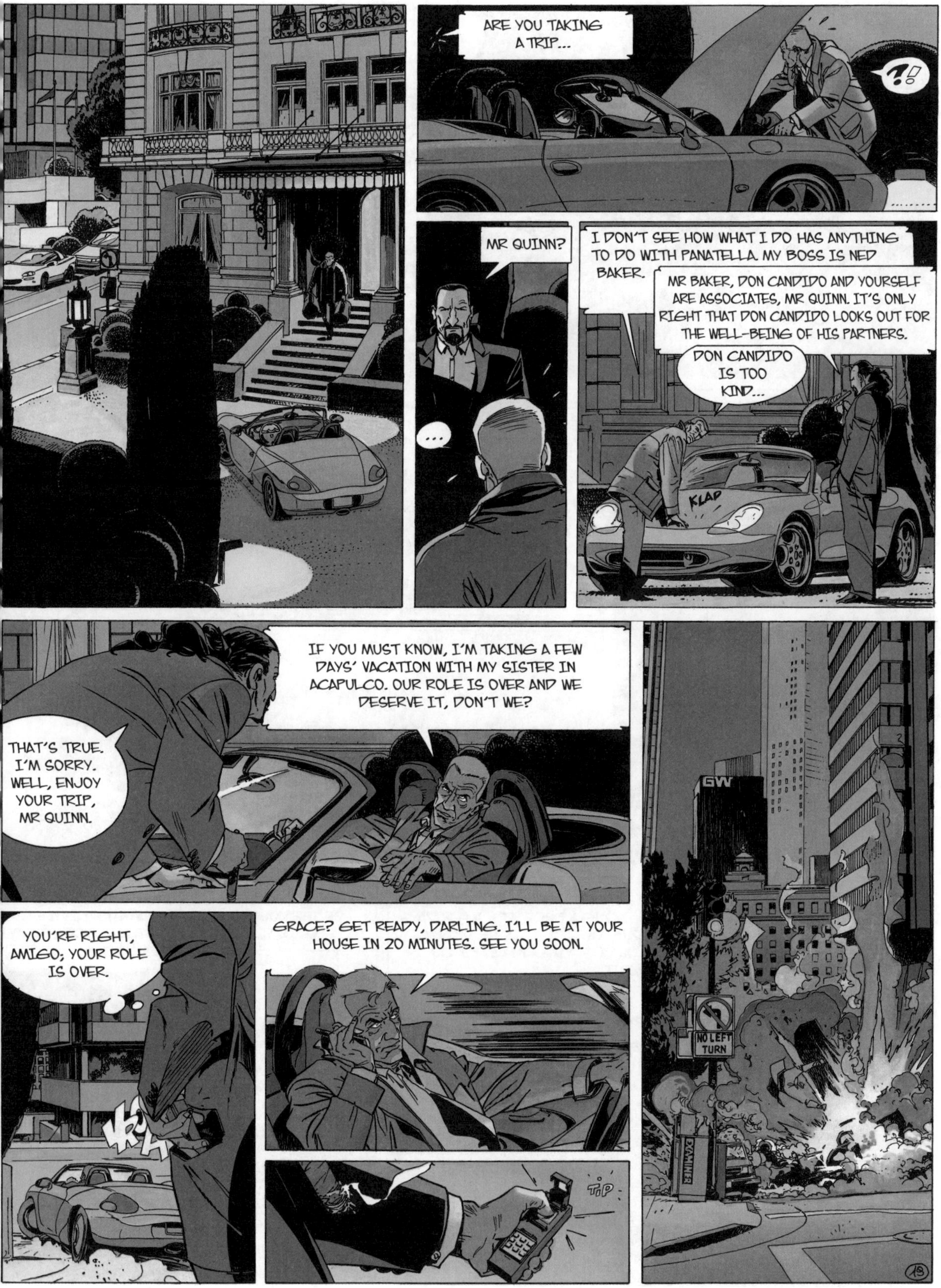
ARE YOU TAKING A TRIP...
?!
MR QUINN?
...
I DON'T SEE HOW WHAT I DO HAS ANYTHING TO DO WITH PANATELLA. MY BOSS IS NED BAKER.
MR BAKER, DON CANDIDO AND YOURSELF ARE ASSOCIATES, MR QUINN. IT'S ONLY RIGHT THAT DON CANDIDO LOOKS OUT FOR THE WELL-BEING OF HIS PARTNERS.
DON CANDIDO IS TOO KIND...
KLAP
IF YOU MUST KNOW, I'M TAKING A FEW DAYS' VACATION WITH MY SISTER IN ACAPULCO. OUR ROLE IS OVER AND WE DESERVE IT, DON'T WE?
THAT'S TRUE. I'M SORRY. WELL, ENJOY YOUR TRIP, MR QUINN.
YOU'RE RIGHT, AMIGO; YOUR ROLE IS OVER.
GRACE? GET READY, DARLING. I'LL BE AT YOUR HOUSE IN 20 MINUTES. SEE YOU SOON.
TIP
GW
NO LEFT TURN
EXAMINER
19

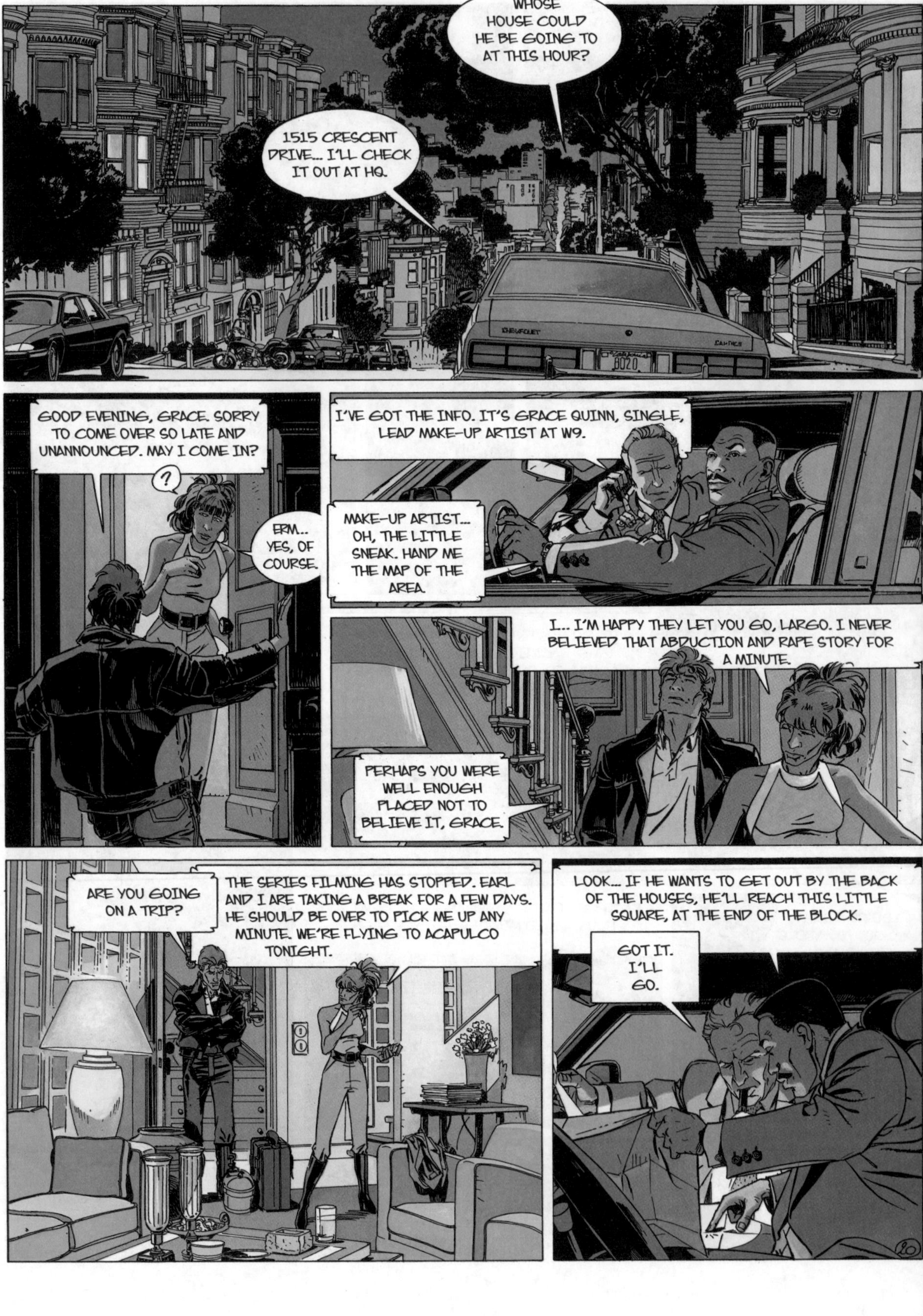
WHOSE HOUSE COULD HE BE GOING TO AT THIS HOUR?
1515 CRESCENT DRIVE... I'LL CHECK IT OUT AT HQ.
GOOD EVENING, GRACE. SORRY TO COME OVER SO LATE AND UNANNOUNCED. MAY I COME IN?
?
ERM... YES, OF COURSE.
I'VE GOT THE INFO. IT'S GRACE QUINN, SINGLE, LEAD MAKE-UP ARTIST AT W9.
MAKE-UP ARTIST... OH, THE LITTLE SNEAK. HAND ME THE MAP OF THE AREA.
I... I'M HAPPY THEY LET YOU GO, LARGO. I NEVER BELIEVED THAT ABDUCTION AND RAPE STORY FOR A MINUTE.
PERHAPS YOU WERE WELL ENOUGH PLACED NOT TO BELIEVE IT, GRACE.
ARE YOU GOING ON A TRIP?
THE SERIES FILMING HAS STOPPED. EARL AND I ARE TAKING A BREAK FOR A FEW DAYS. HE SHOULD BE OVER TO PICK ME UP ANY MINUTE. WE'RE FLYING TO ACAPULCO TONIGHT.
LOOK... IF HE WANTS TO GET OUT BY THE BACK OF THE HOUSES, HE'LL REACH THIS LITTLE SQUARE, AT THE END OF THE BLOCK.
GOT IT. I'LL GO.
20

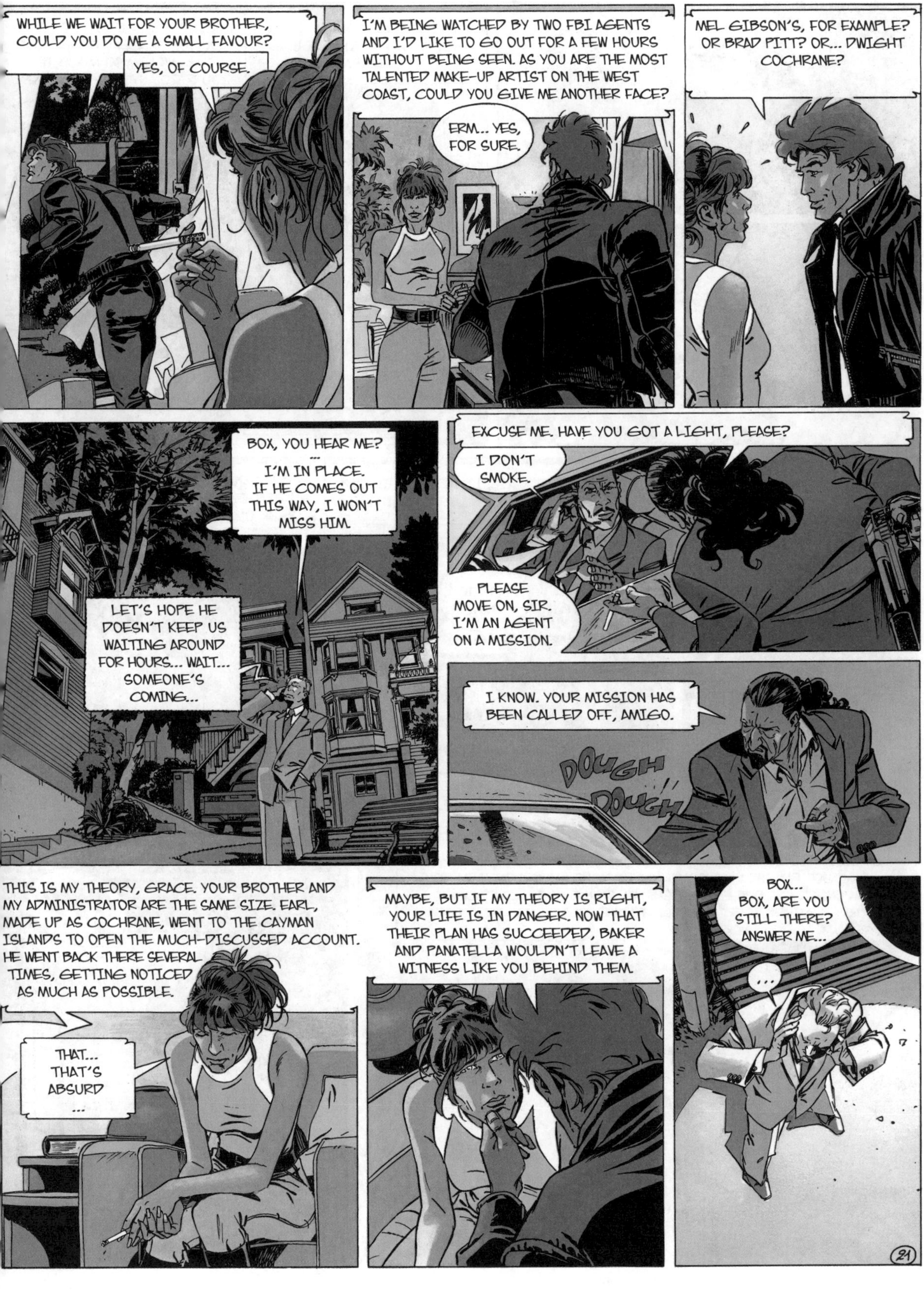
WHILE WE WAIT FOR YOUR BROTHER, COULD YOU DO ME A SMALL FAVOUR?
YES, OF COURSE.
I'M BEING WATCHED BY TWO FBI AGENTS AND I'D LIKE TO GO OUT FOR A FEW HOURS WITHOUT BEING SEEN. AS YOU ARE THE MOST TALENTED MAKE-UP ARTIST ON THE WEST COAST, COULD YOU GIVE ME ANOTHER FACE?
ERM... YES, FOR SURE.
MEL GIBSON'S, FOR EXAMPLE? OR BRAD PITT? OR... DWIGHT COCHRANE?
BOX, YOU HEAR ME? ... I'M IN PLACE. IF HE COMES OUT THIS WAY, I WON'T MISS HIM.
LET'S HOPE HE DOESN'T KEEP US WAITING AROUND FOR HOURS... WAIT... SOMEONE'S COMING...
EXCUSE ME. HAVE YOU GOT A LIGHT, PLEASE?
I DON'T SMOKE.
PLEASE MOVE ON, SIR. I'M AN AGENT ON A MISSION.
I KNOW. YOUR MISSION HAS BEEN CALLED OFF, AMIGO.
DOUGH
DOUGH
THIS IS MY THEORY, GRACE. YOUR BROTHER AND MY ADMINISTRATOR ARE THE SAME SIZE. EARL, MADE UP AS COCHRANE, WENT TO THE CAYMAN ISLANDS TO OPEN THE MUCH-DISCUSSED ACCOUNT. HE WENT BACK THERE SEVERAL TIMES, GETTING NOTICED AS MUCH AS POSSIBLE.
THAT... THAT'S ABSURD ...
MAYBE, BUT IF MY THEORY IS RIGHT, YOUR LIFE IS IN DANGER. NOW THAT THEIR PLAN HAS SUCCEEDED, BAKER AND PANATELLA WOULDN'T LEAVE A WITNESS LIKE YOU BEHIND THEM.
BOX... BOX, ARE YOU STILL THERE? ANSWER ME...
...
21

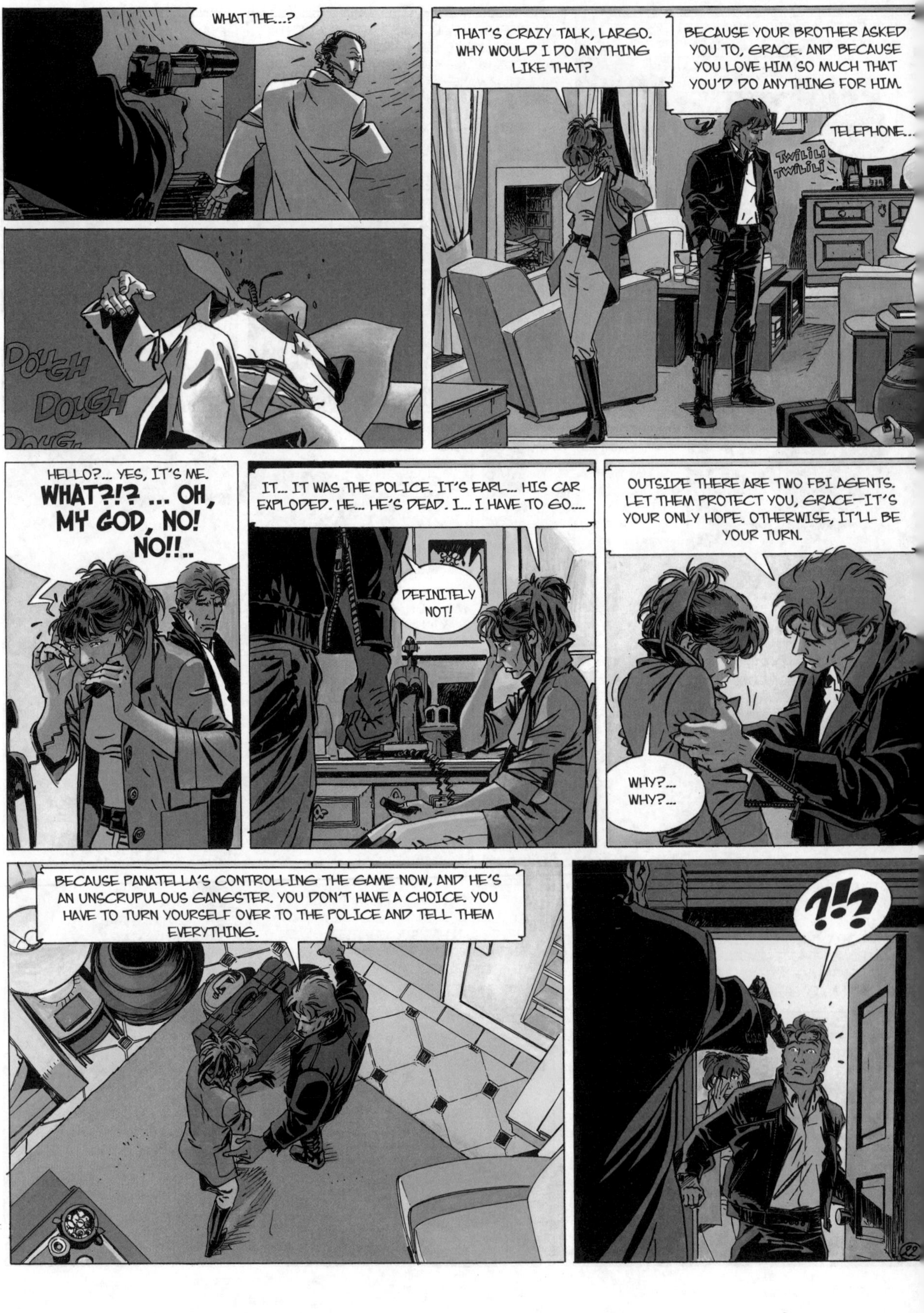
WHAT THE...?
DOUGH
DOUGH
THAT'S CRAZY TALK, LARGO. WHY WOULD I DO ANYTHING LIKE THAT?
BECAUSE YOUR BROTHER ASKED YOU TO, GRACE. AND BECAUSE YOU LOVE HIM SO MUCH THAT YOU'D DO ANYTHING FOR HIM.
TWILILI TWILILI
TELEPHONE...
HELLO?... YES, IT'S ME. WHAT?!? ... OH, MY GOD, NO! NO!!..
IT... IT WAS THE POLICE. IT'S EARL... HIS CAR EXPLODED. HE... HE'S DEAD. I... I HAVE TO GO....
DEFINITELY NOT!
OUTSIDE THERE ARE TWO FBI AGENTS. LET THEM PROTECT YOU, GRACE—IT'S YOUR ONLY HOPE. OTHERWISE, IT'LL BE YOUR TURN.
WHY?... WHY?...
BECAUSE PANATELLA'S CONTROLLING THE GAME NOW, AND HE'S AN UNSCRUPULOUS GANGSTER. YOU DON'T HAVE A CHOICE. YOU HAVE TO TURN YOURSELF OVER TO THE POLICE AND TELL THEM EVERYTHING.
?!?
22

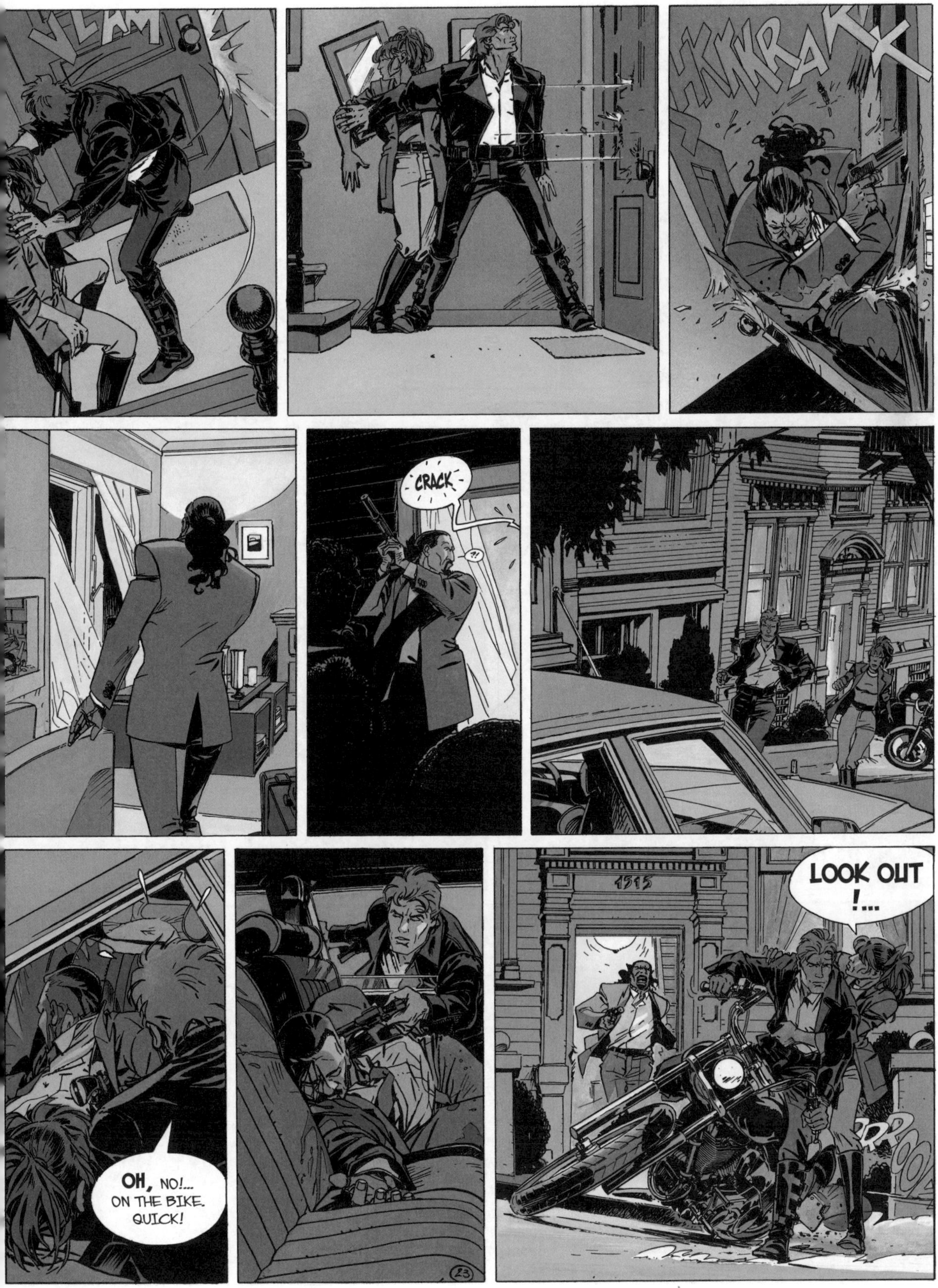
CRACK
?!
OH, NO!...
ON THE BIKE.
QUICK!
LOOK OUT
!...

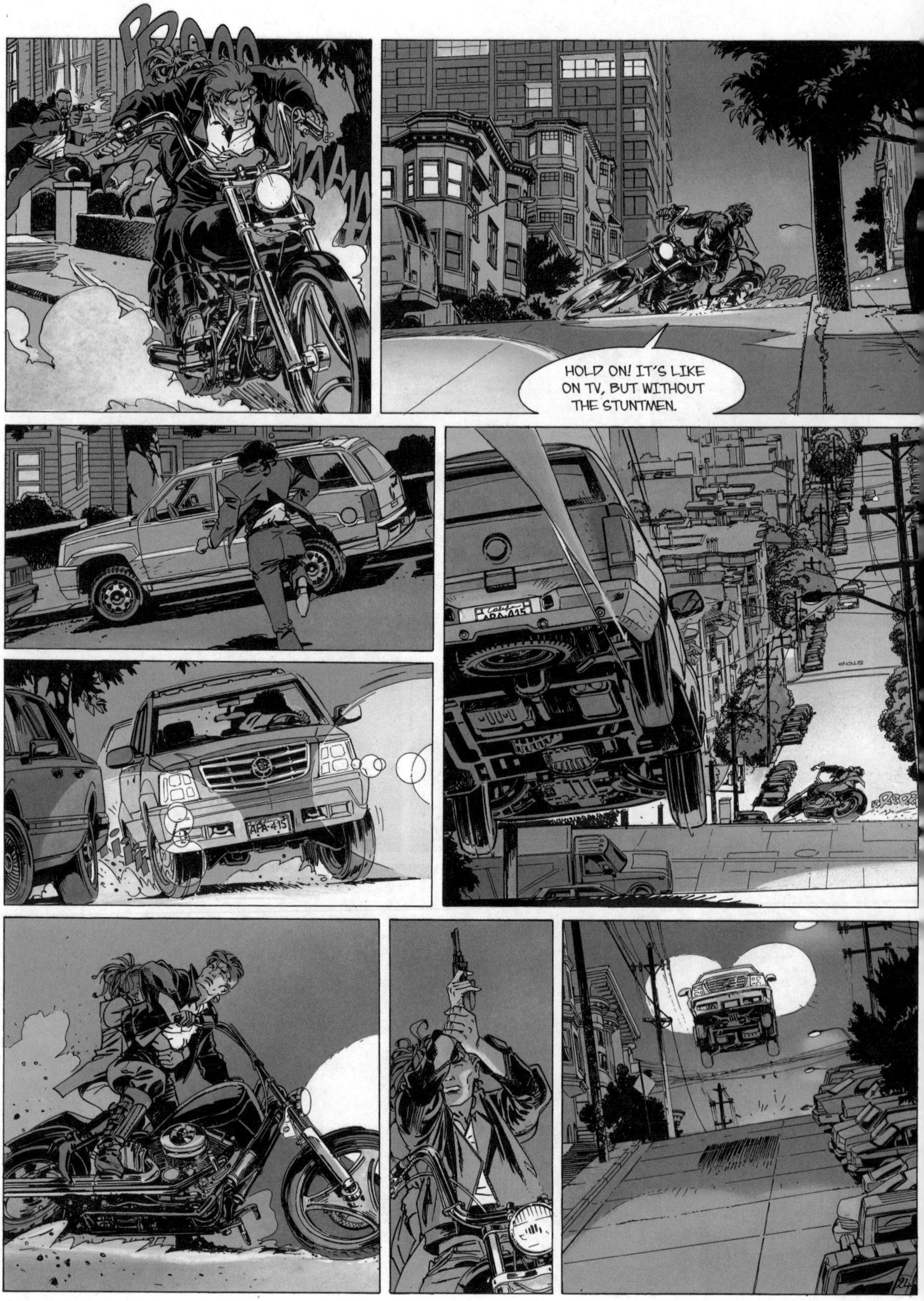
PRAOOO
AAAAAA
HOLD ON! IT'S LIKE ON TV, BUT WITHOUT THE STUNTMEN.
APA-415
STOP
APA-415

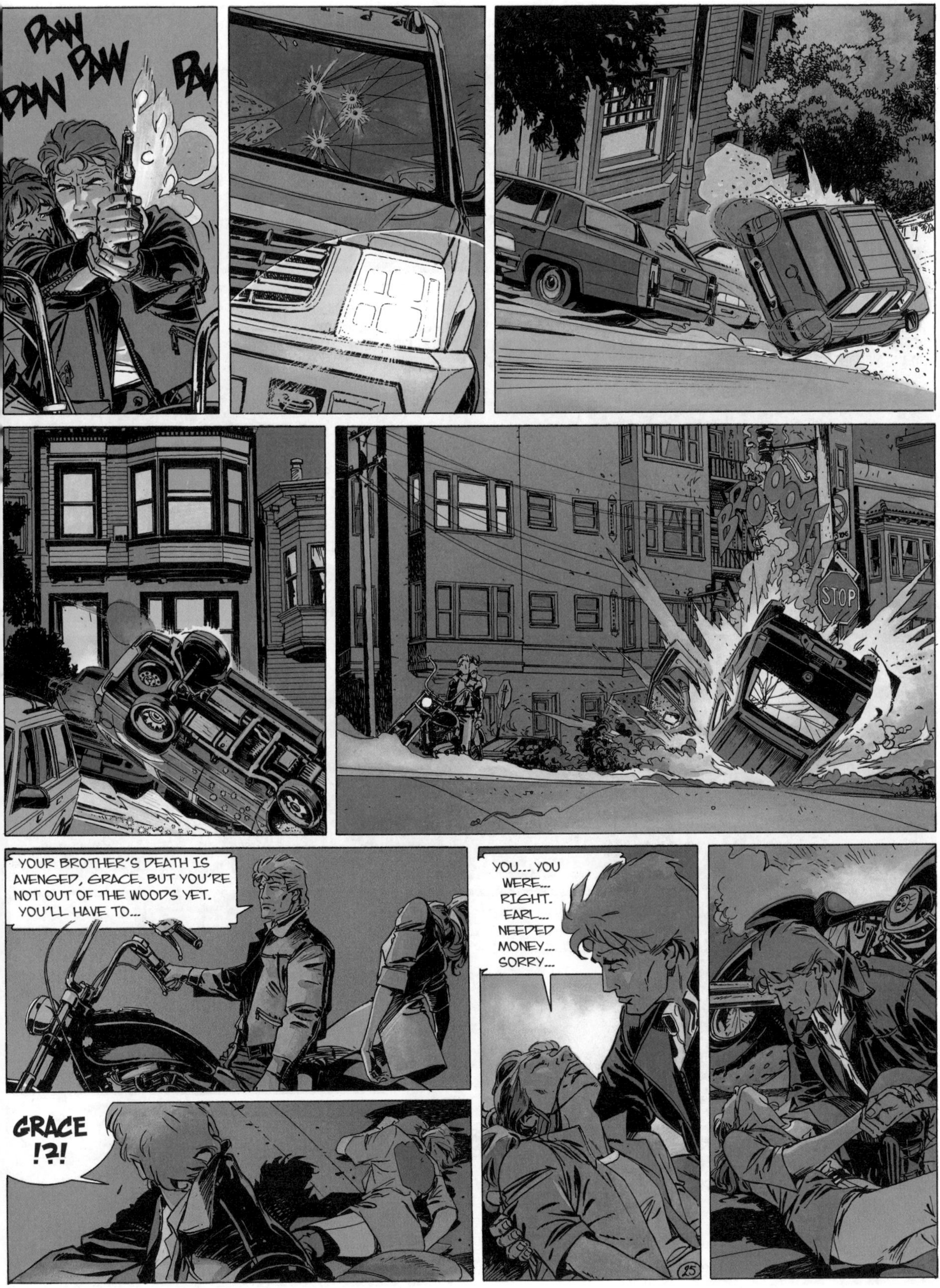
PAW
PAW PAW
PAW
BROOOF
STOP
YOUR BROTHER'S DEATH IS AVENGED, GRACE. BUT YOU'RE NOT OUT OF THE WOODS YET. YOU'LL HAVE TO...
GRACE !?!
YOU... YOU WERE... RIGHT. EARL... NEEDED MONEY... SORRY...

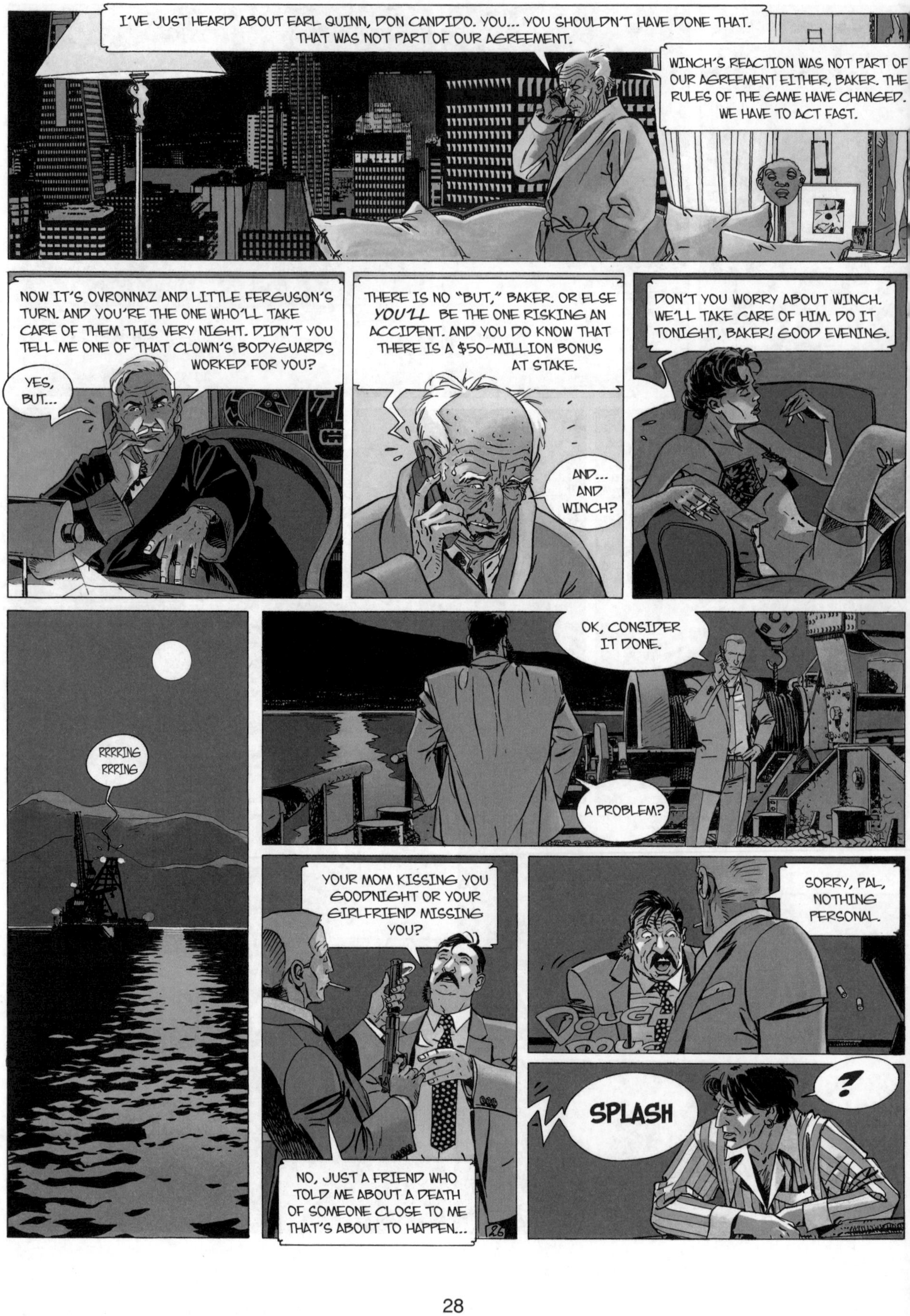
I'VE JUST HEARD ABOUT EARL QUINN, DON CANDIDO. YOU... YOU SHOULDN'T HAVE DONE THAT. THAT WAS NOT PART OF OUR AGREEMENT.
WINCH'S REACTION WAS NOT PART OF OUR AGREEMENT EITHER, BAKER. THE RULES OF THE GAME HAVE CHANGED. WE HAVE TO ACT FAST.
NOW IT'S OVRONNAZ AND LITTLE FERGUSON'S TURN. AND YOU'RE THE ONE WHO'LL TAKE CARE OF THEM THIS VERY NIGHT. DIDN'T YOU TELL ME ONE OF THAT CLOWN'S BODYGUARDS WORKED FOR YOU?
YES, BUT...
THERE IS NO "BUT," BAKER. OR ELSE *YOU'LL* BE THE ONE RISKING AN ACCIDENT. AND YOU DO KNOW THAT THERE IS A $50-MILLION BONUS AT STAKE.
AND... AND WINCH?
DON'T YOU WORRY ABOUT WINCH. WE'LL TAKE CARE OF HIM. DO IT TONIGHT, BAKER! GOOD EVENING.
RRRRING RRRING
OK, CONSIDER IT DONE.
A PROBLEM?
YOUR MOM KISSING YOU GOODNIGHT OR YOUR GIRLFRIEND MISSING YOU?
NO, JUST A FRIEND WHO TOLD ME ABOUT A DEATH OF SOMEONE CLOSE TO ME THAT'S ABOUT TO HAPPEN...
SORRY, PAL, NOTHING PERSONAL.
SPLASH
?

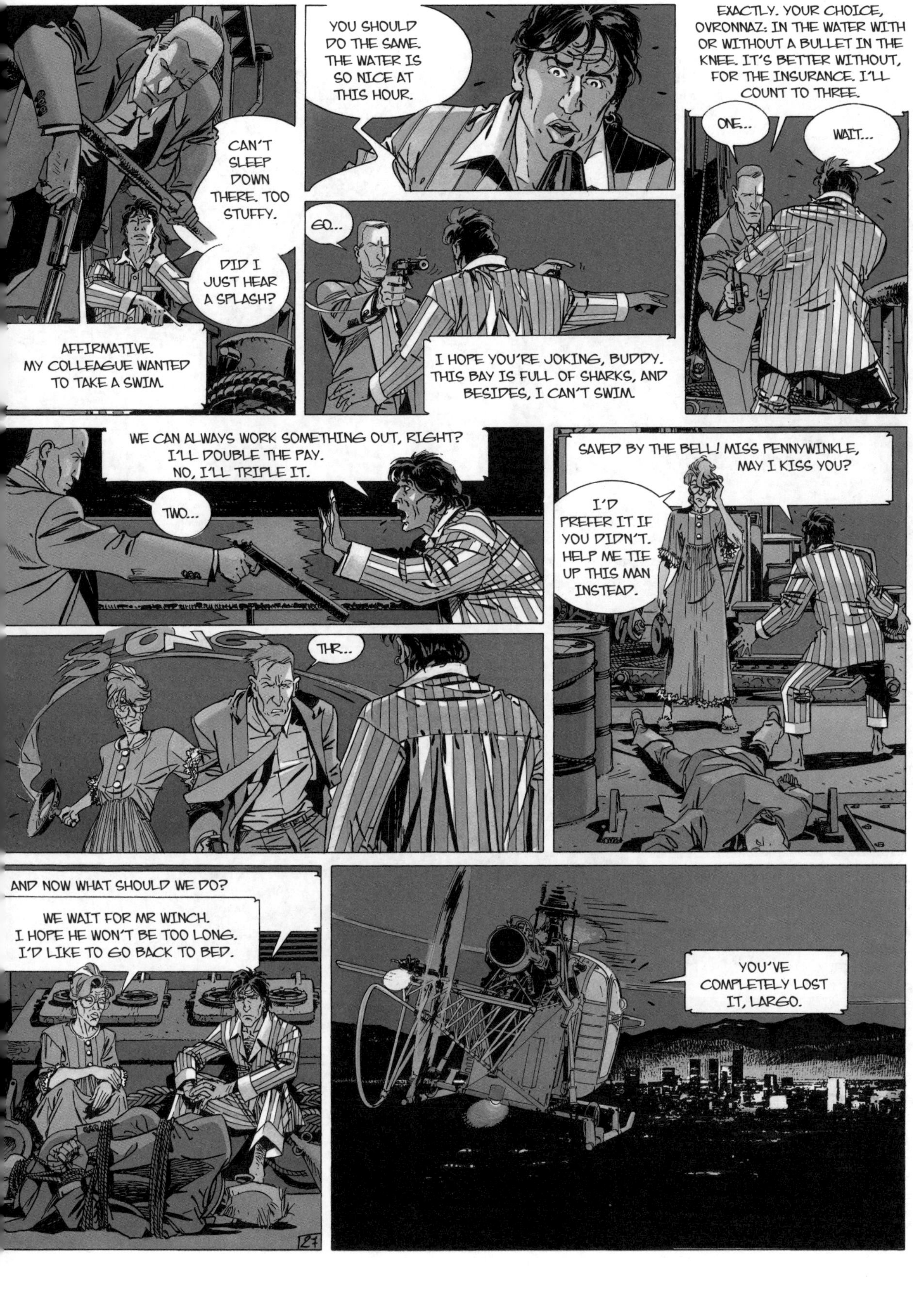
CAN'T SLEEP DOWN THERE. TOO STUFFY.
DID I JUST HEAR A SPLASH?
AFFIRMATIVE. MY COLLEAGUE WANTED TO TAKE A SWIM.
YOU SHOULD DO THE SAME. THE WATER IS SO NICE AT THIS HOUR.
GO...
I HOPE YOU'RE JOKING, BUDDY. THIS BAY IS FULL OF SHARKS, AND BESIDES, I CAN'T SWIM.
EXACTLY. YOUR CHOICE, OVRONNAZ: IN THE WATER WITH OR WITHOUT A BULLET IN THE KNEE. IT'S BETTER WITHOUT, FOR THE INSURANCE. I'LL COUNT TO THREE.
ONE...
WAIT...
WE CAN ALWAYS WORK SOMETHING OUT, RIGHT? I'LL DOUBLE THE PAY. NO, I'LL TRIPLE IT.
TWO...
BONG
THR...
SAVED BY THE BELL! MISS PENNYWINKLE, MAY I KISS YOU?
I'D PREFER IT IF YOU DIDN'T. HELP ME TIE UP THIS MAN INSTEAD.
AND NOW WHAT SHOULD WE DO?
WE WAIT FOR MR WINCH. I HOPE HE WON'T BE TOO LONG. I'D LIKE TO GO BACK TO BED.
27
YOU'VE COMPLETELY LOST IT, LARGO.

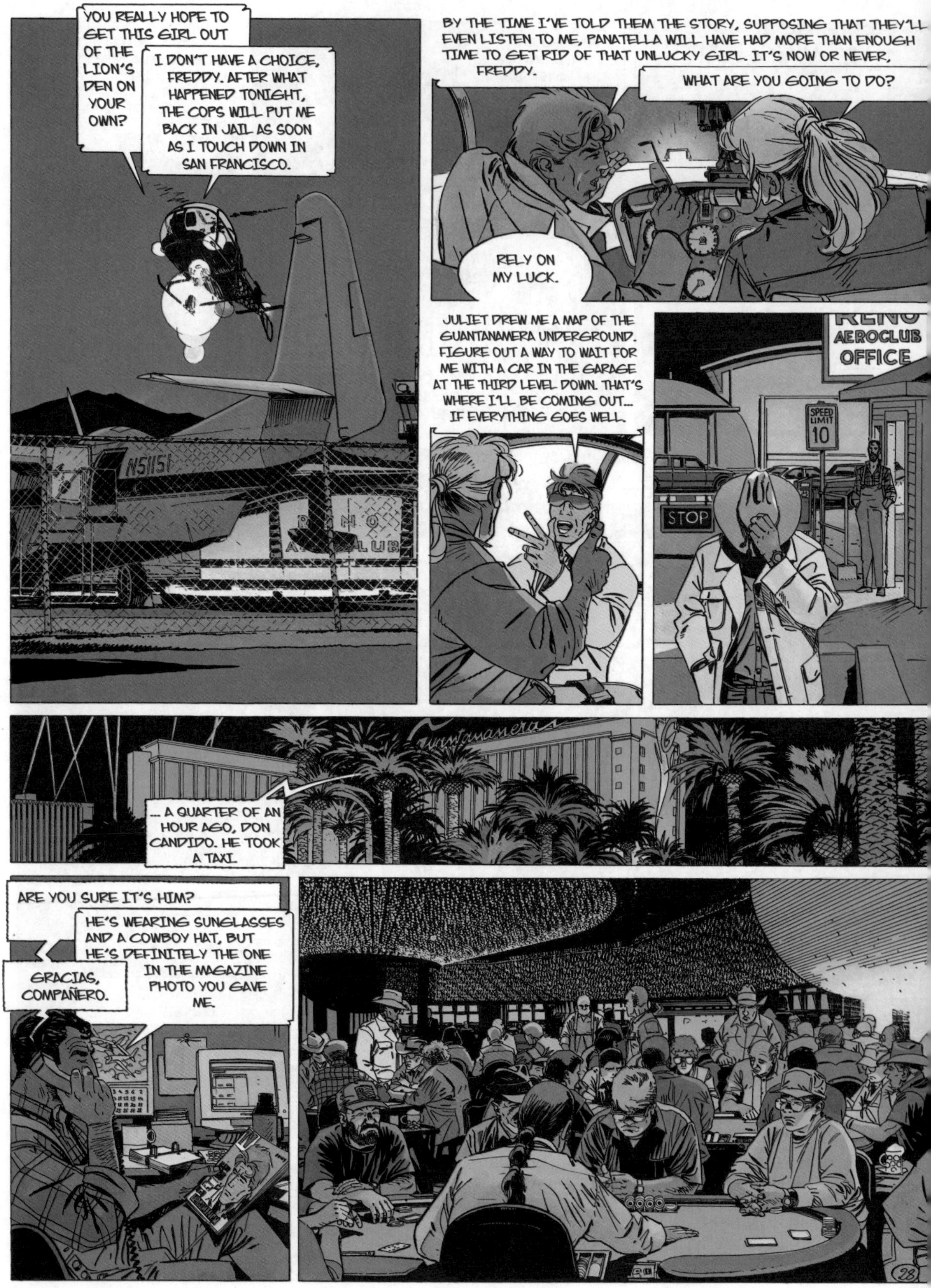
YOU REALLY HOPE TO GET THIS GIRL OUT OF THE LION'S DEN ON YOUR OWN?
I DON'T HAVE A CHOICE, FREDDY. AFTER WHAT HAPPENED TONIGHT, THE COPS WILL PUT ME BACK IN JAIL AS SOON AS I TOUCH DOWN IN SAN FRANCISCO.
N5151
RENO AEROCLUB
BY THE TIME I'VE TOLD THEM THE STORY, SUPPOSING THAT THEY'LL EVEN LISTEN TO ME, PANATELLA WILL HAVE HAD MORE THAN ENOUGH TIME TO GET RID OF THAT UNLUCKY GIRL. IT'S NOW OR NEVER, FREDDY.
WHAT ARE YOU GOING TO DO?
RELY ON MY LUCK.
JULIET DREW ME A MAP OF THE GUANTANAMERA UNDERGROUND. FIGURE OUT A WAY TO WAIT FOR ME WITH A CAR IN THE GARAGE AT THE THIRD LEVEL DOWN. THAT'S WHERE I'LL BE COMING OUT... IF EVERYTHING GOES WELL.
RENO AEROCLUB OFFICE
SPEED LIMIT 10
STOP
Guantanamera
... A QUARTER OF AN HOUR AGO, DON CANDIDO. HE TOOK A TAXI.
ARE YOU SURE IT'S HIM?
HE'S WEARING SUNGLASSES AND A COWBOY HAT, BUT HE'S DEFINITELY THE ONE IN THE MAGAZINE PHOTO YOU GAVE ME.
GRACIAS, COMPAÑERO.
28

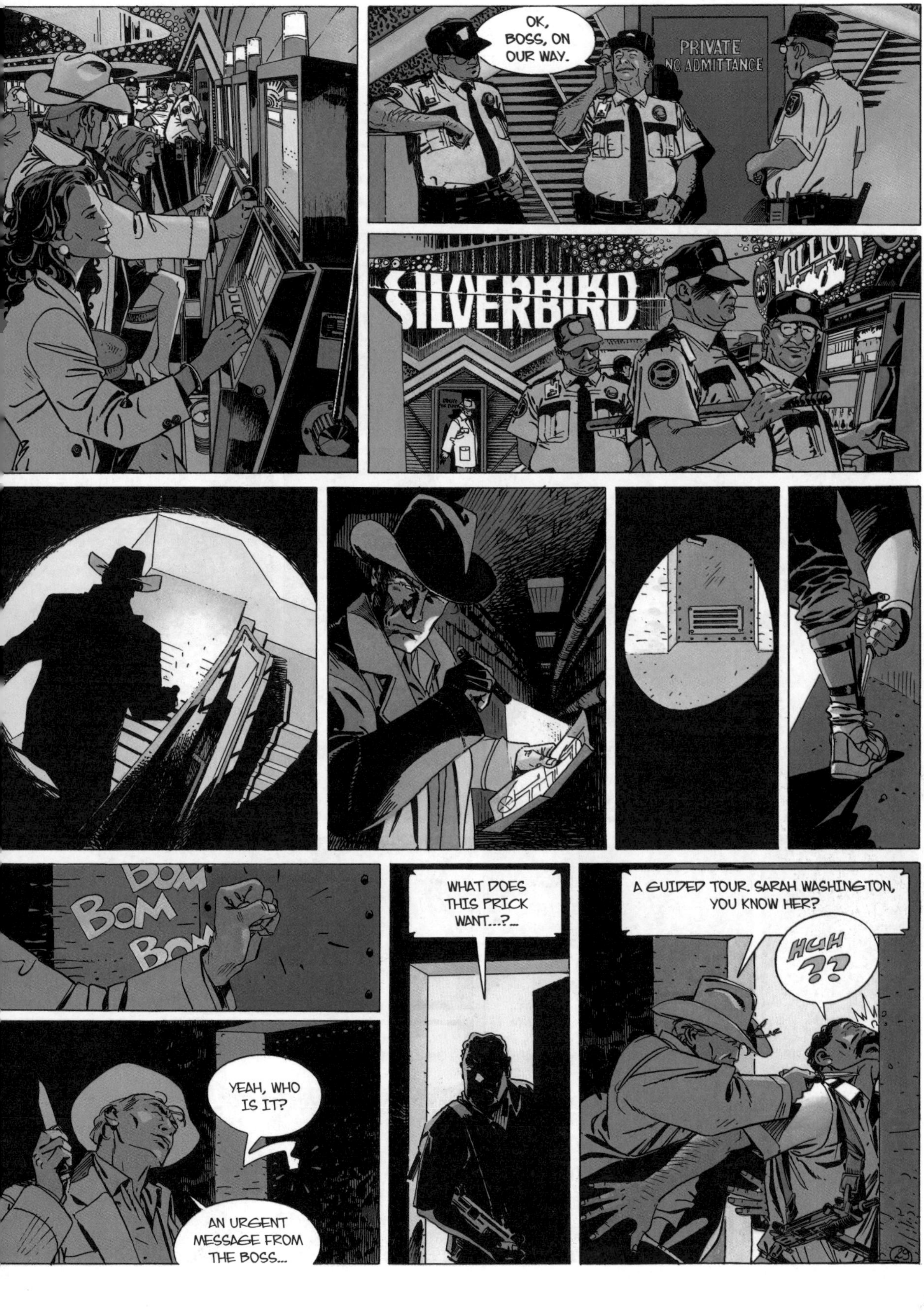
OK, BOSS, ON OUR WAY.
PRIVATE
NO ADMITTANCE
SILVERBIRD
BOM
BOM
YEAH, WHO IS IT?
AN URGENT MESSAGE FROM THE BOSS...
WHAT DOES THIS PRICK WANT...?...
A GUIDED TOUR. SARAH WASHINGTON, YOU KNOW HER?
HUH ??

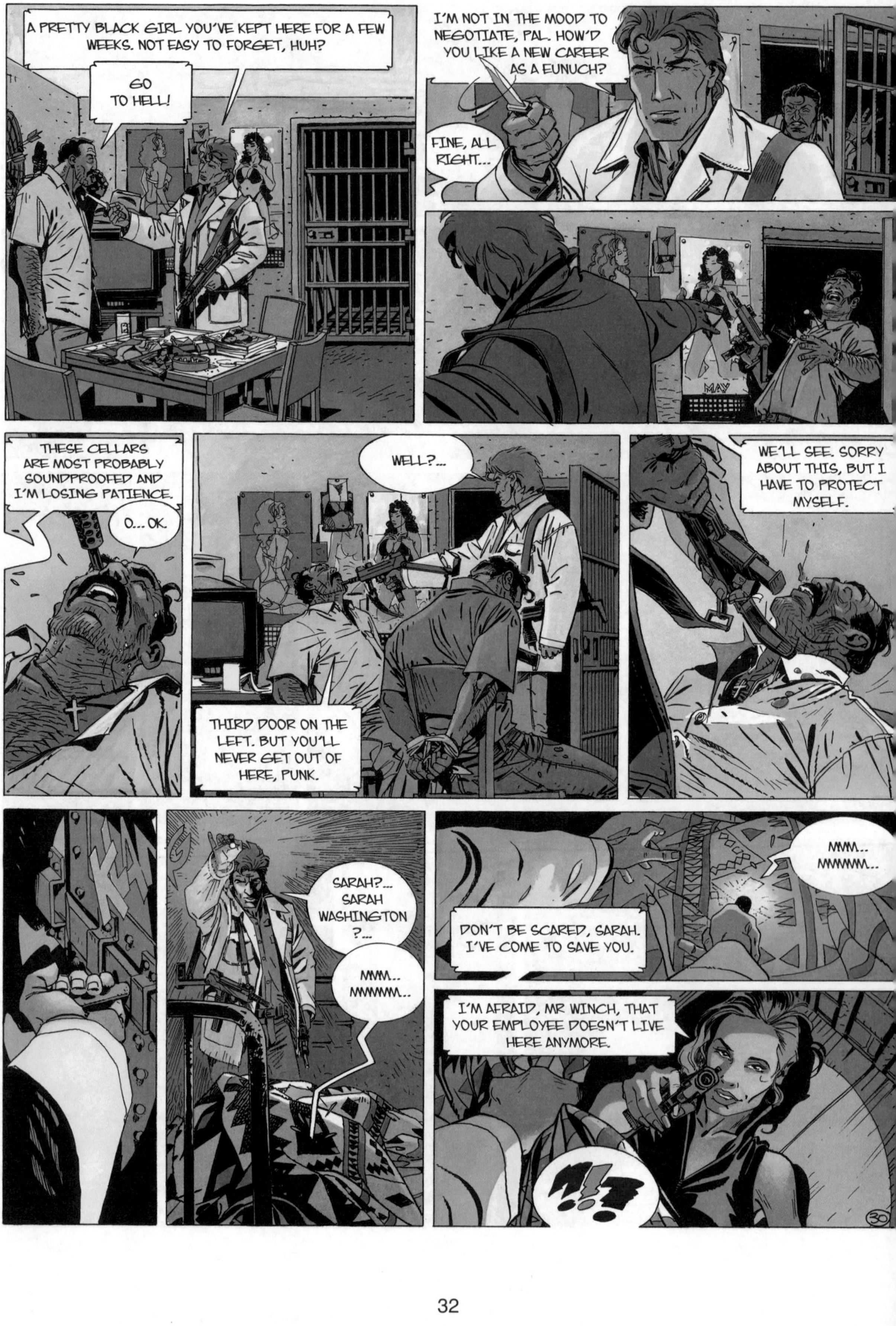
A PRETTY BLACK GIRL YOU'VE KEPT HERE FOR A FEW WEEKS. NOT EASY TO FORGET, HUH?
GO TO HELL!
I'M NOT IN THE MOOD TO NEGOTIATE, PAL. HOW'D YOU LIKE A NEW CAREER AS A EUNUCH?
FINE, ALL RIGHT...
MAY
THESE CELLARS ARE MOST PROBABLY SOUNDPROOFED AND I'M LOSING PATIENCE.
O... OK.
WELL?...
THIRD DOOR ON THE LEFT. BUT YOU'LL NEVER GET OUT OF HERE, PUNK.
WE'LL SEE. SORRY ABOUT THIS, BUT I HAVE TO PROTECT MYSELF.
KLAN
SARAH?... SARAH WASHINGTON ?...
MMM... MMMMM...
MMM... MMMMM...
DON'T BE SCARED, SARAH. I'VE COME TO SAVE YOU.
I'M AFRAID, MR WINCH, THAT YOUR EMPLOYEE DOESN'T LIVE HERE ANYMORE.
!!?
30

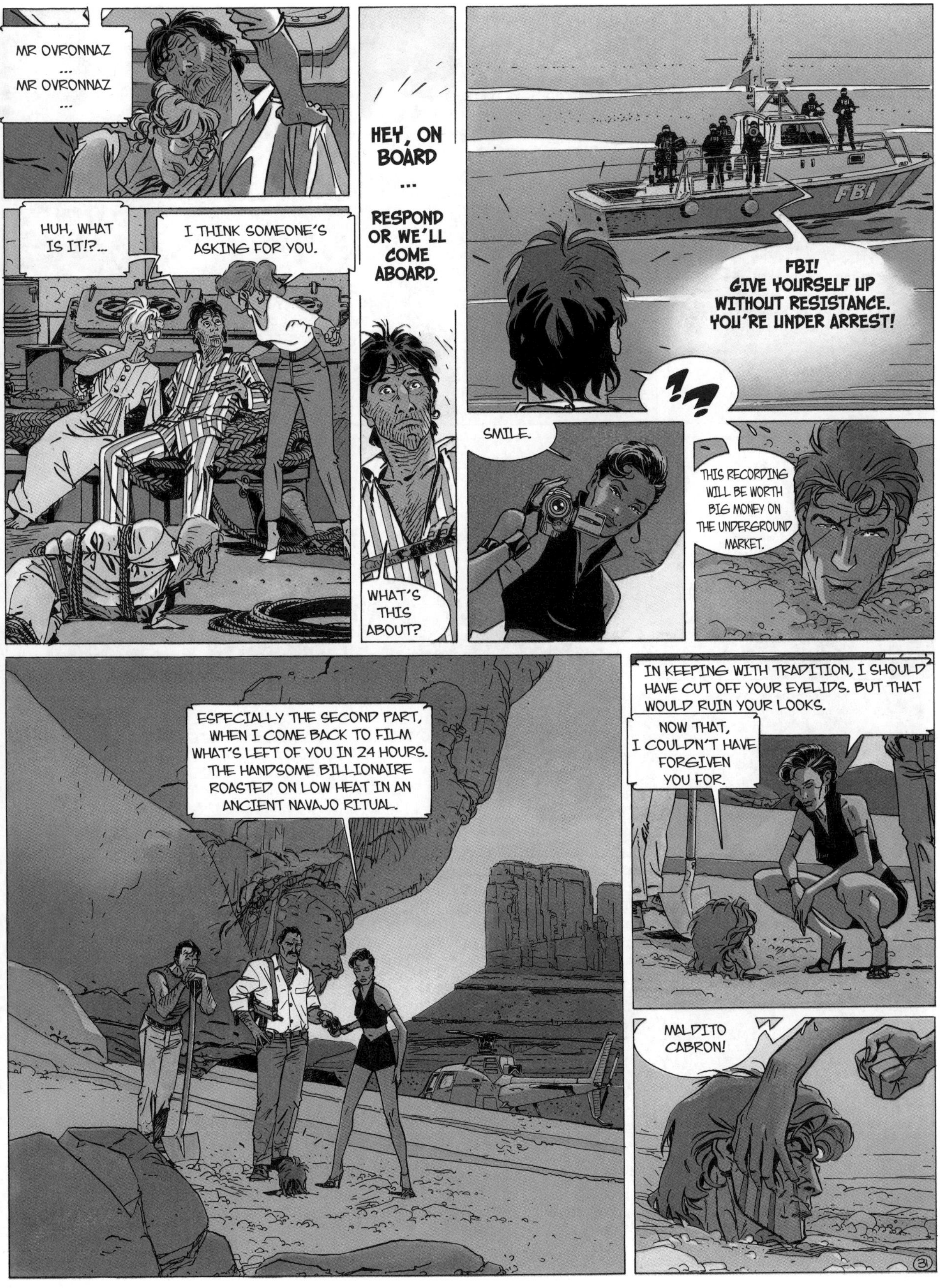
MR OVRONNAZ
...
MR OVRONNAZ
...
HEY, ON BOARD
...
RESPOND OR WE'LL COME ABOARD.
FBI! GIVE YOURSELF UP WITHOUT RESISTANCE. YOU'RE UNDER ARREST!
HUH, WHAT IS IT!?...
I THINK SOMEONE'S ASKING FOR YOU.
WHAT'S THIS ABOUT?
!?
SMILE.
THIS RECORDING WILL BE WORTH BIG MONEY ON THE UNDERGROUND MARKET.
ESPECIALLY THE SECOND PART, WHEN I COME BACK TO FILM WHAT'S LEFT OF YOU IN 24 HOURS. THE HANDSOME BILLIONAIRE ROASTED ON LOW HEAT IN AN ANCIENT NAVAJO RITUAL.
IN KEEPING WITH TRADITION, I SHOULD HAVE CUT OFF YOUR EYELIDS. BUT THAT WOULD RUIN YOUR LOOKS.
NOW THAT, I COULDN'T HAVE FORGIVEN YOU FOR.
MALDITO CABRON!
31

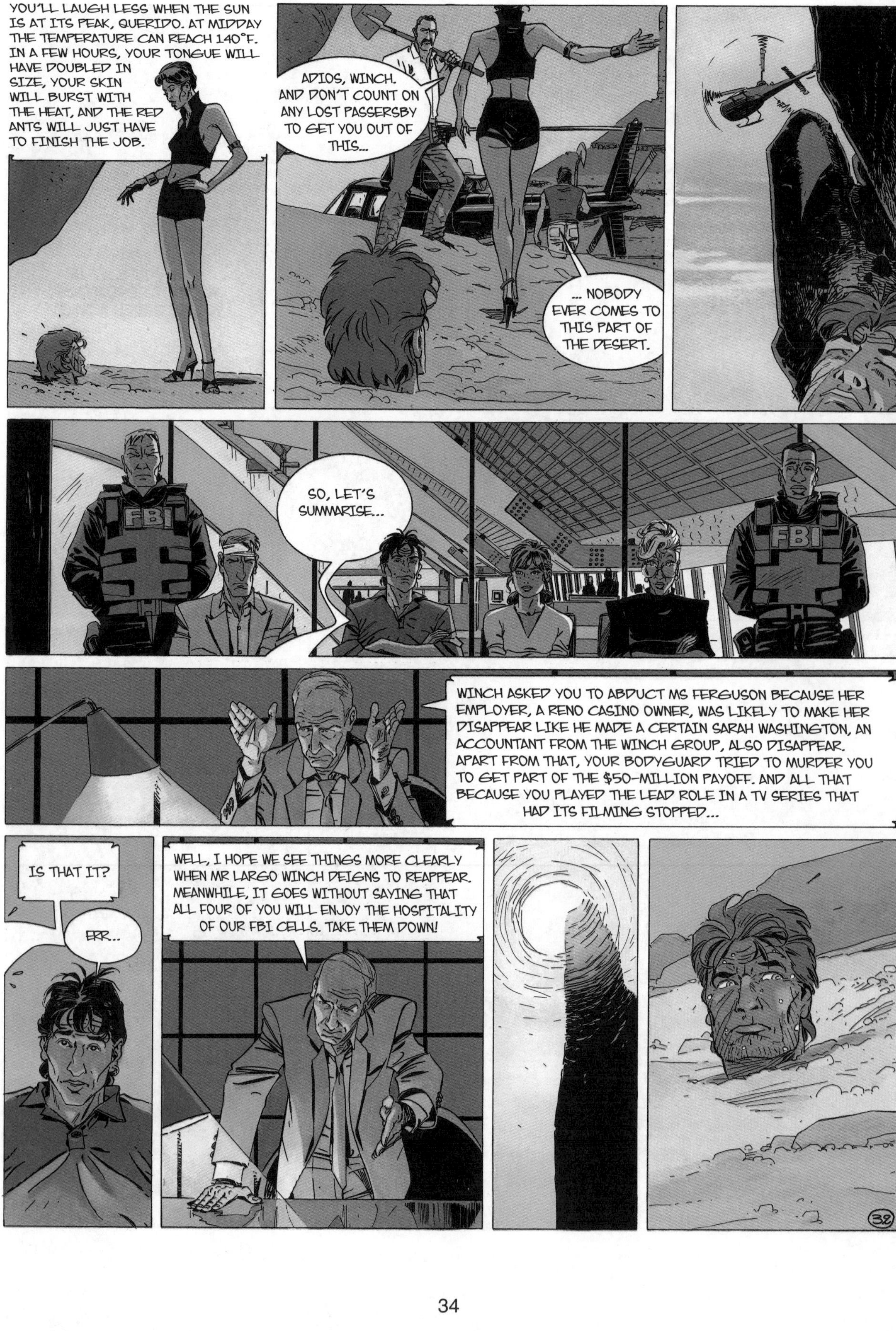
YOU'LL LAUGH LESS WHEN THE SUN IS AT ITS PEAK, QUERIDO. AT MIDDAY THE TEMPERATURE CAN REACH 140°F. IN A FEW HOURS, YOUR TONGUE WILL HAVE DOUBLED IN SIZE, YOUR SKIN WILL BURST WITH THE HEAT, AND THE RED ANTS WILL JUST HAVE TO FINISH THE JOB.
ADIOS, WINCH. AND DON'T COUNT ON ANY LOST PASSERSBY TO GET YOU OUT OF THIS...
... NOBODY EVER COMES TO THIS PART OF THE DESERT.
SO, LET'S SUMMARISE...
WINCH ASKED YOU TO ABDUCT MS FERGUSON BECAUSE HER EMPLOYER, A RENO CASINO OWNER, WAS LIKELY TO MAKE HER DISAPPEAR LIKE HE MADE A CERTAIN SARAH WASHINGTON, AN ACCOUNTANT FROM THE WINCH GROUP, ALSO DISAPPEAR. APART FROM THAT, YOUR BODYGUARD TRIED TO MURDER YOU TO GET PART OF THE $50-MILLION PAYOFF. AND ALL THAT BECAUSE YOU PLAYED THE LEAD ROLE IN A TV SERIES THAT HAD ITS FILMING STOPPED...
IS THAT IT?
ERR...
WELL, I HOPE WE SEE THINGS MORE CLEARLY WHEN MR LARGO WINCH DEIGNS TO REAPPEAR. MEANWHILE, IT GOES WITHOUT SAYING THAT ALL FOUR OF YOU WILL ENJOY THE HOSPITALITY OF OUR FBI CELLS. TAKE THEM DOWN!
32

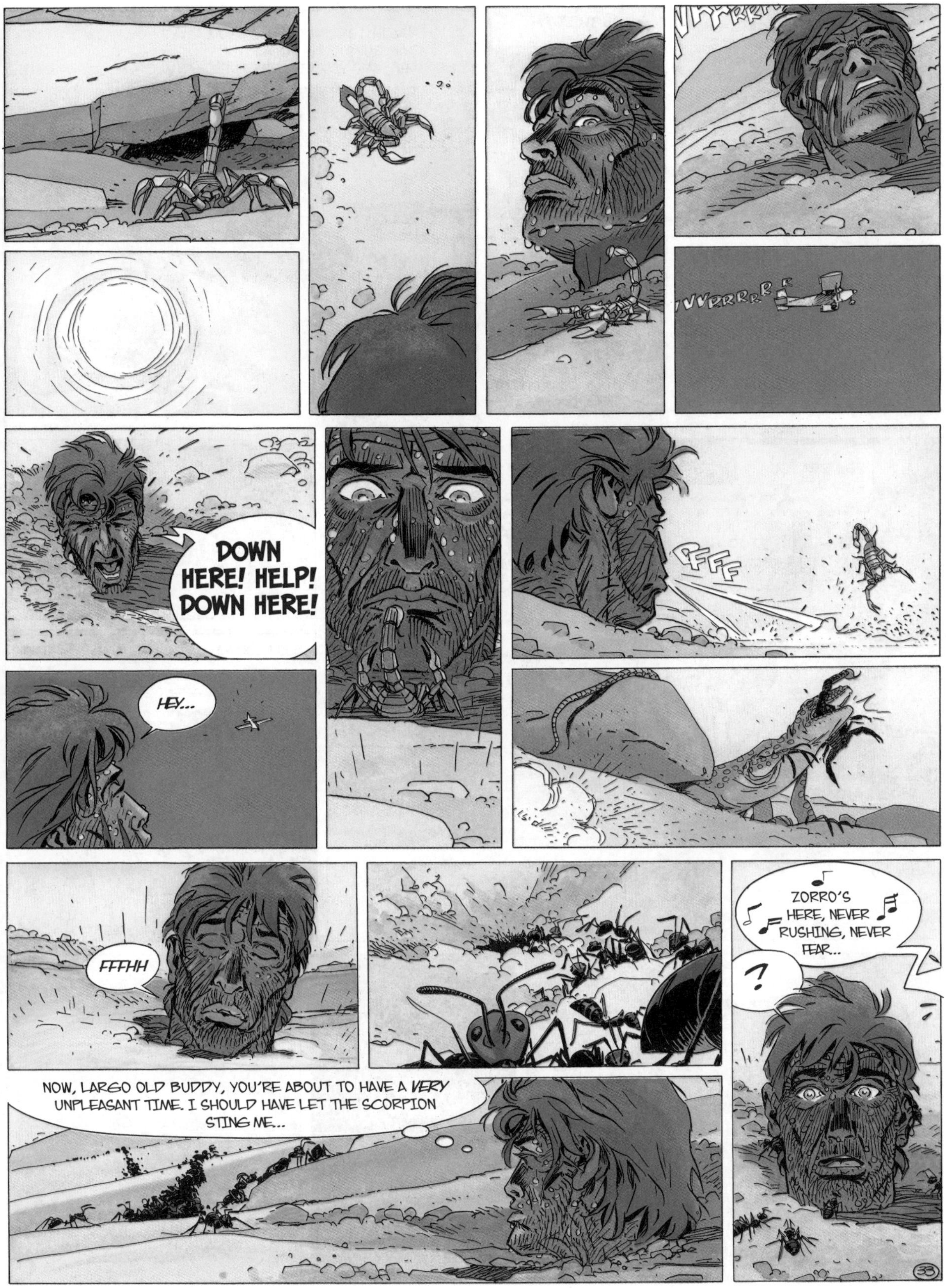
DOWN HERE! HELP! DOWN HERE!
HEY...
FFFHH
ZORRO'S HERE, NEVER RUSHING, NEVER FEAR...
?
NOW, LARGO OLD BUDDY, YOU'RE ABOUT TO HAVE A *VERY* UNPLEASANT TIME. I SHOULD HAVE LET THE SCORPION STING ME...
33

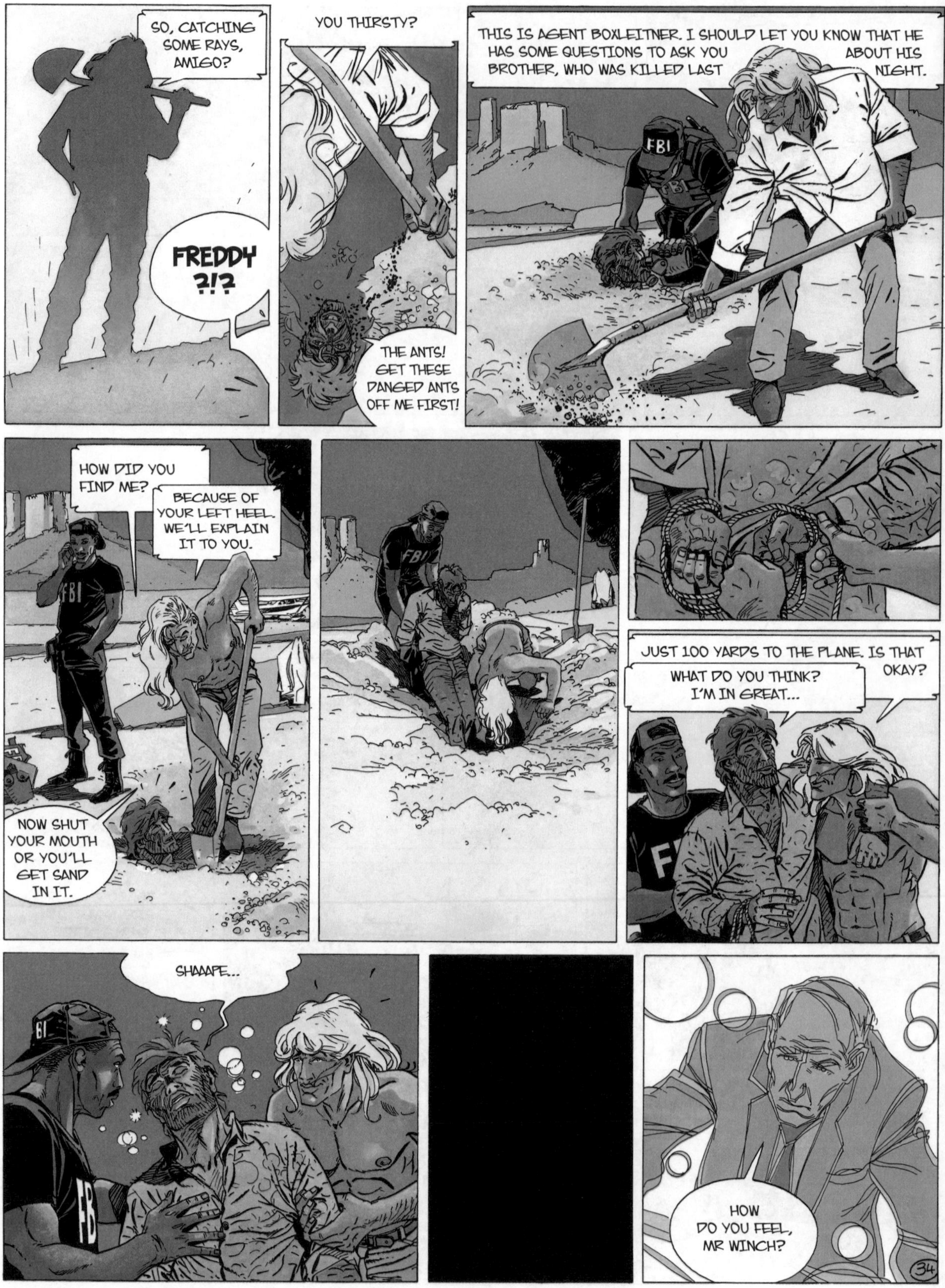

SO, CATCHING SOME RAYS, AMIGO?
FREDDY ?!?
YOU THIRSTY?
THE ANTS! GET THESE DANGED ANTS OFF ME FIRST!
THIS IS AGENT BOXLEITNER. I SHOULD LET YOU KNOW THAT HE HAS SOME QUESTIONS TO ASK YOU ABOUT HIS BROTHER, WHO WAS KILLED LAST NIGHT.
FBI
HOW DID YOU FIND ME?
BECAUSE OF YOUR LEFT HEEL. WE'LL EXPLAIN IT TO YOU.
NOW SHUT YOUR MOUTH OR YOU'LL GET SAND IN IT.
JUST 100 YARDS TO THE PLANE. IS THAT OKAY?
WHAT DO YOU THINK? I'M IN GREAT...
SHAAAPE...
HOW DO YOU FEEL, MR WINCH?
34

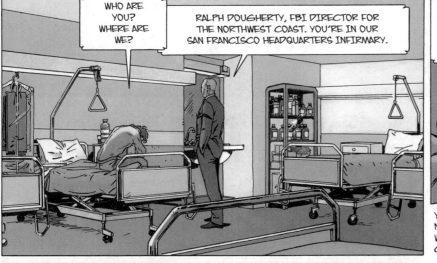

WHO ARE YOU? WHERE ARE WE?

RALPH DOUGHERTY, FBI DIRECTOR FOR THE NORTHWEST COAST. YOU'RE IN OUR SAN FRANCISCO HEADQUARTERS INFIRMARY.

YOU WERE LUCKY... YOU MADE IT THROUGH WITH JUST EXTREME SUNSTROKE. DO YOU FEEL ABLE TO ANSWER A FEW QUESTIONS?

YES, BUT NOT HERE. WHERE ARE MY CLOTHES?

HERE THEY ARE, WASHED AND IRONED. OF COURSE, WE TOOK OUT THE TRACKER THAT WE'D PUT IN YOUR LEFT SHOE HEEL BEFORE YOU LEFT PRISON.

TRACKER?...

A CLASSIC MINIATURISED TRANSMITTER ALLOWED US TO FIND YOU WITHIN A RADIUS OF FIVE MILES. YOU CAN THANK US. IT'S ON ACCOUNT OF THAT TRACKER THAT WE WERE ABLE TO FIND YOU SO EASILY.

YOUR PILOT, FREDDY KAPLAN, WAS WAITING FOR YOU IN THE PARKING GARAGE OF THE GUANTANAMERA, JUST AS YOU ASKED HIM TO. WHEN HE DIDN'T HEAR FROM YOU, HE UNDERSTOOD THAT YOU'D FAILED AND THAT HE WAS IN DANGER HIMSELF. BEING JUSTIFIABLY WARY OF THE RENO POLICE, HE HAD THE BRIGHT IDEA OF CONTACTING US.

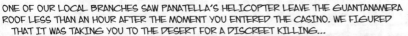

ONE OF OUR LOCAL BRANCHES SAW PANATELLA'S HELICOPTER LEAVE THE GUANTANAMERA ROOF LESS THAN AN HOUR AFTER THE MOMENT YOU ENTERED THE CASINO. WE FIGURED THAT IT WAS TAKING YOU TO THE DESERT FOR A DISCREET KILLING...

... YOU KNOW THE REST.

AND NOW, MR WINCH, I'D LIKE YOU TO TELL ME ABOUT THE MURDER, LAST NIGHT, OF MY TWO AGENTS WHO HAD YOU UNDER SURVEILLANCE, DAWSON AND BOXLEITNER.

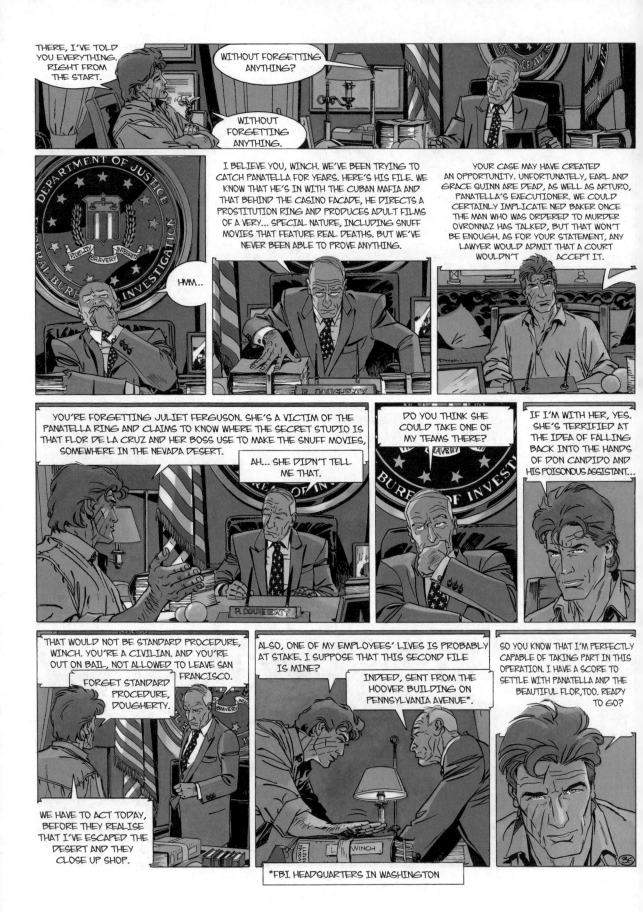

THERE, I'VE TOLD YOU EVERYTHING. RIGHT FROM THE START.

WITHOUT FORGETTING ANYTHING?

WITHOUT FORGETTING ANYTHING.

I BELIEVE YOU, WINCH. WE'VE BEEN TRYING TO CATCH PANATELLA FOR YEARS. HERE'S HIS FILE. WE KNOW THAT HE'S IN WITH THE CUBAN MAFIA AND THAT BEHIND THE CASINO FACADE, HE DIRECTS A PROSTITUTION RING AND PRODUCES ADULT FILMS OF A VERY... SPECIAL NATURE, INCLUDING SNUFF MOVIES THAT FEATURE REAL DEATHS. BUT WE'VE NEVER BEEN ABLE TO PROVE ANYTHING.

YOUR CASE MAY HAVE CREATED AN OPPORTUNITY. UNFORTUNATELY, EARL AND GRACE QUINN ARE DEAD, AS WELL AS ARTURO, PANATELLA'S EXECUTIONER. WE COULD CERTAINLY IMPLICATE NED BAKER ONCE THE MAN WHO WAS ORDERED TO MURDER OVRONNAZ HAS TALKED, BUT THAT WON'T BE ENOUGH. AS FOR YOUR STATEMENT, ANY LAWYER WOULD ADMIT THAT A COURT WOULDN'T ACCEPT IT.

HMM...

YOU'RE FORGETTING JULIET FERGUSON. SHE'S A VICTIM OF THE PANATELLA RING AND CLAIMS TO KNOW WHERE THE SECRET STUDIO IS THAT FLOR DE LA CRUZ AND HER BOSS USE TO MAKE THE SNUFF MOVIES, SOMEWHERE IN THE NEVADA DESERT.

AH... SHE DIDN'T TELL ME THAT.

DO YOU THINK SHE COULD TAKE ONE OF MY TEAMS THERE?

IF I'M WITH HER, YES. SHE'S TERRIFIED AT THE IDEA OF FALLING BACK INTO THE HANDS OF DON CANDIDO AND HIS POISONOUS ASSISTANT...

THAT WOULD NOT BE STANDARD PROCEDURE, WINCH. YOU'RE A CIVILIAN. AND YOU'RE OUT ON BAIL, NOT ALLOWED TO LEAVE SAN FRANCISCO.

FORGET STANDARD PROCEDURE, DOUGHERTY.

WE HAVE TO ACT TODAY, BEFORE THEY REALISE THAT I'VE ESCAPED THE DESERT AND THEY CLOSE UP SHOP.

ALSO, ONE OF MY EMPLOYEES' LIVES IS PROBABLY AT STAKE. I SUPPOSE THAT THIS SECOND FILE IS MINE?

INDEED, SENT FROM THE HOOVER BUILDING ON PENNSYLVANIA AVENUE*.

SO YOU KNOW THAT I'M PERFECTLY CAPABLE OF TAKING PART IN THIS OPERATION. I HAVE A SCORE TO SETTLE WITH PANATELLA AND THE BEAUTIFUL FLOR, TOO. READY TO GO?

*FBI HEADQUARTERS IN WASHINGTON

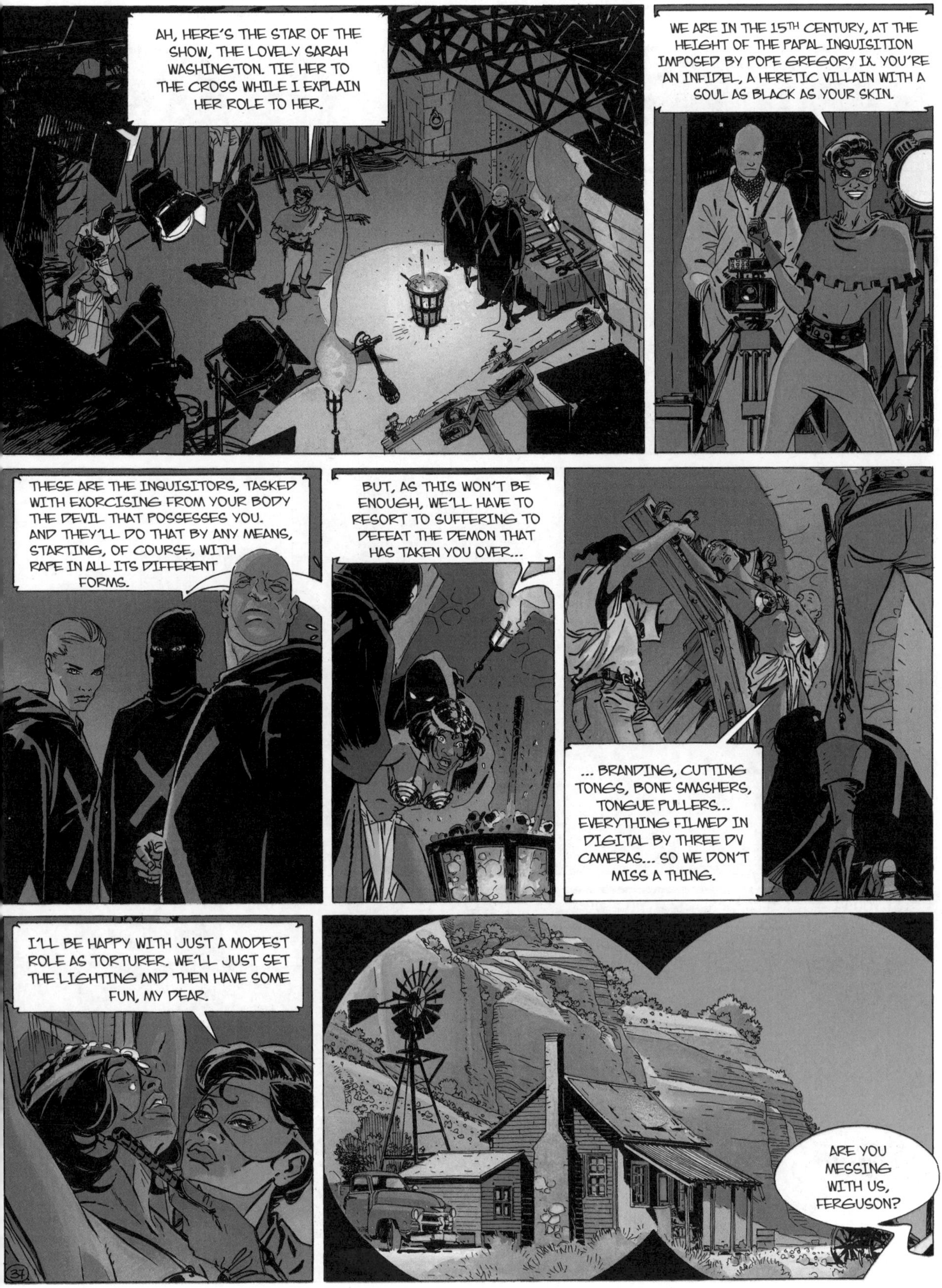
AH, HERE'S THE STAR OF THE SHOW, THE LOVELY SARAH WASHINGTON. TIE HER TO THE CROSS WHILE I EXPLAIN HER ROLE TO HER.
WE ARE IN THE 15TH CENTURY, AT THE HEIGHT OF THE PAPAL INQUISITION IMPOSED BY POPE GREGORY IX. YOU'RE AN INFIDEL, A HERETIC VILLAIN WITH A SOUL AS BLACK AS YOUR SKIN.
THESE ARE THE INQUISITORS, TASKED WITH EXORCISING FROM YOUR BODY THE DEVIL THAT POSSESSES YOU. AND THEY'LL DO THAT BY ANY MEANS, STARTING, OF COURSE, WITH RAPE IN ALL ITS DIFFERENT FORMS.
BUT, AS THIS WON'T BE ENOUGH, WE'LL HAVE TO RESORT TO SUFFERING TO DEFEAT THE DEMON THAT HAS TAKEN YOU OVER...
... BRANDING, CUTTING TONGS, BONE SMASHERS, TONGUE PULLERS... EVERYTHING FILMED IN DIGITAL BY THREE DV CAMERAS... SO WE DON'T MISS A THING.
I'LL BE HAPPY WITH JUST A MODEST ROLE AS TORTURER. WE'LL JUST SET THE LIGHTING AND THEN HAVE SOME FUN, MY DEAR.
ARE YOU MESSING WITH US, FERGUSON?

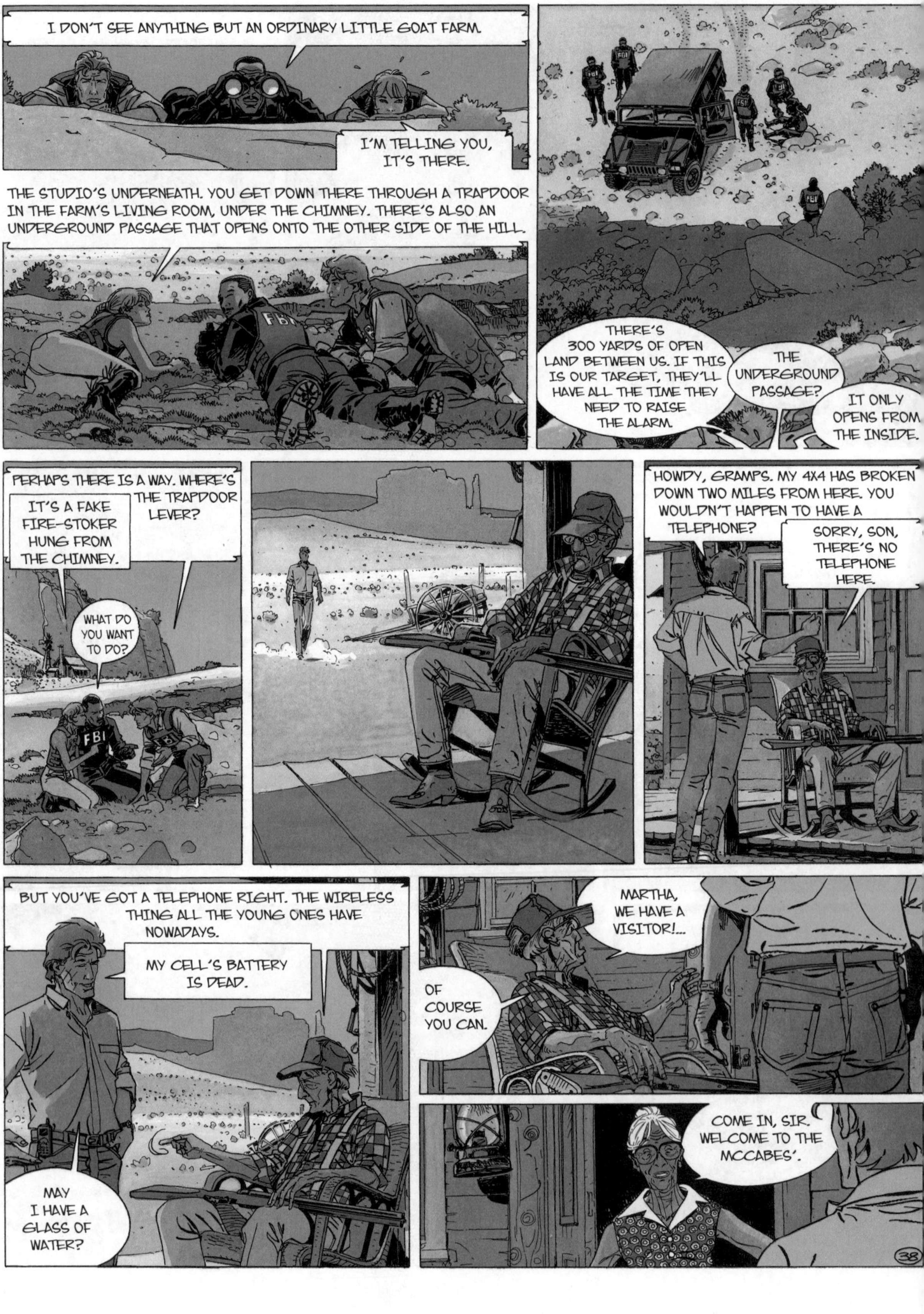

I DON'T SEE ANYTHING BUT AN ORDINARY LITTLE GOAT FARM.
I'M TELLING YOU, IT'S THERE.
THE STUDIO'S UNDERNEATH. YOU GET DOWN THERE THROUGH A TRAPDOOR IN THE FARM'S LIVING ROOM, UNDER THE CHIMNEY. THERE'S ALSO AN UNDERGROUND PASSAGE THAT OPENS ONTO THE OTHER SIDE OF THE HILL.
FBI
THERE'S 300 YARDS OF OPEN LAND BETWEEN US. IF THIS IS OUR TARGET, THEY'LL HAVE ALL THE TIME THEY NEED TO RAISE THE ALARM.
THE UNDERGROUND PASSAGE?
IT ONLY OPENS FROM THE INSIDE.
PERHAPS THERE IS A WAY. WHERE'S THE TRAPDOOR LEVER?
IT'S A FAKE FIRE-STOKER HUNG FROM THE CHIMNEY.
WHAT DO YOU WANT TO DO?
HOWDY, GRAMPS. MY 4X4 HAS BROKEN DOWN TWO MILES FROM HERE. YOU WOULDN'T HAPPEN TO HAVE A TELEPHONE?
SORRY, SON, THERE'S NO TELEPHONE HERE.
BUT YOU'VE GOT A TELEPHONE RIGHT. THE WIRELESS THING ALL THE YOUNG ONES HAVE NOWADAYS.
MY CELL'S BATTERY IS DEAD.
MAY I HAVE A GLASS OF WATER?
OF COURSE YOU CAN.
MARTHA, WE HAVE A VISITOR!...
COME IN, SIR. WELCOME TO THE MCCABES'.
38

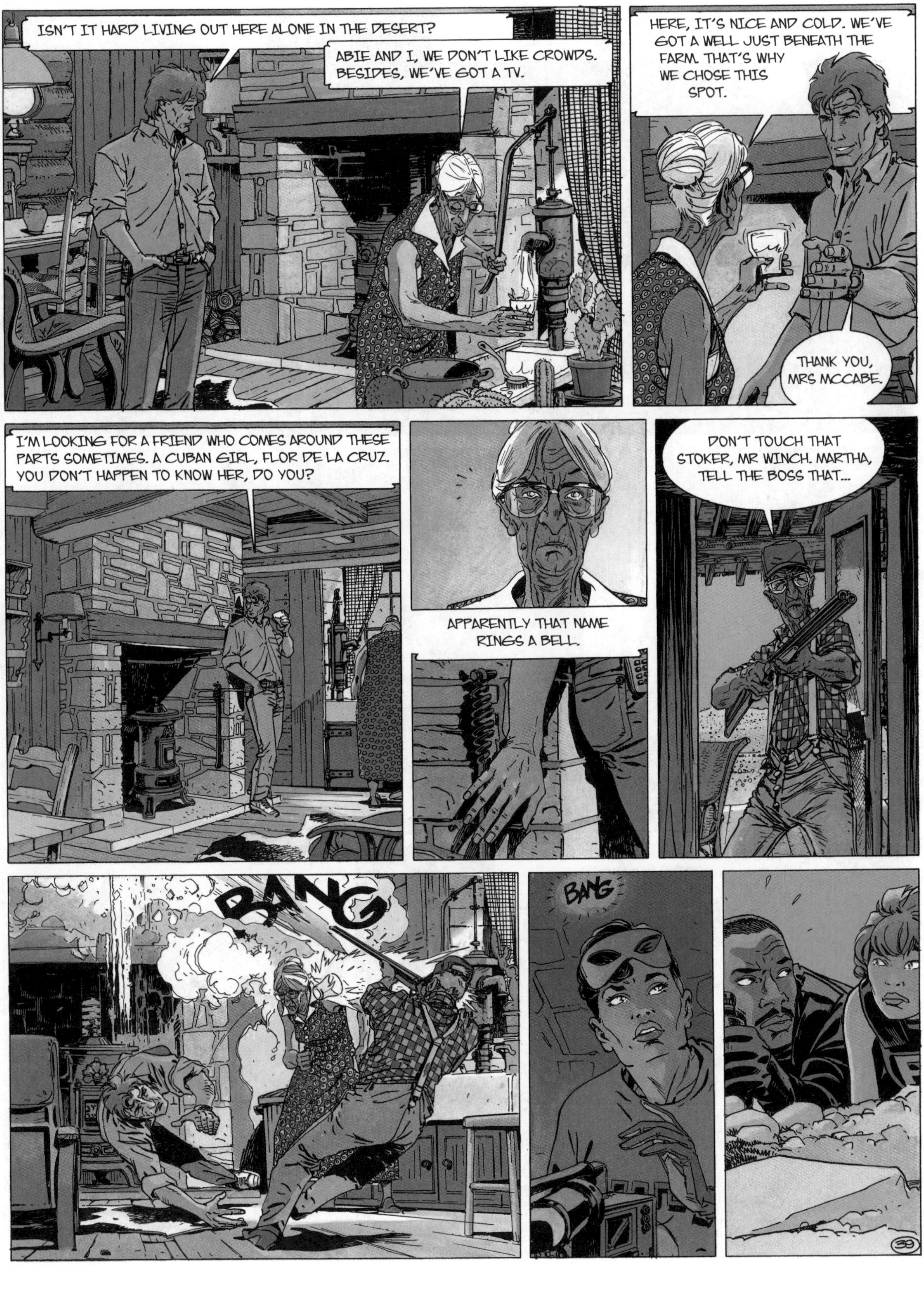
ISN'T IT HARD LIVING OUT HERE ALONE IN THE DESERT?
ABIE AND I, WE DON'T LIKE CROWDS. BESIDES, WE'VE GOT A TV.
HERE, IT'S NICE AND COLD. WE'VE GOT A WELL JUST BENEATH THE FARM. THAT'S WHY WE CHOSE THIS SPOT.
THANK YOU, MRS MCCABE.
I'M LOOKING FOR A FRIEND WHO COMES AROUND THESE PARTS SOMETIMES. A CUBAN GIRL, FLOR DE LA CRUZ. YOU DON'T HAPPEN TO KNOW HER, DO YOU?
APPARENTLY THAT NAME RINGS A BELL.
DON'T TOUCH THAT STOKER, MR WINCH. MARTHA, TELL THE BOSS THAT...
BANG
BANG
39

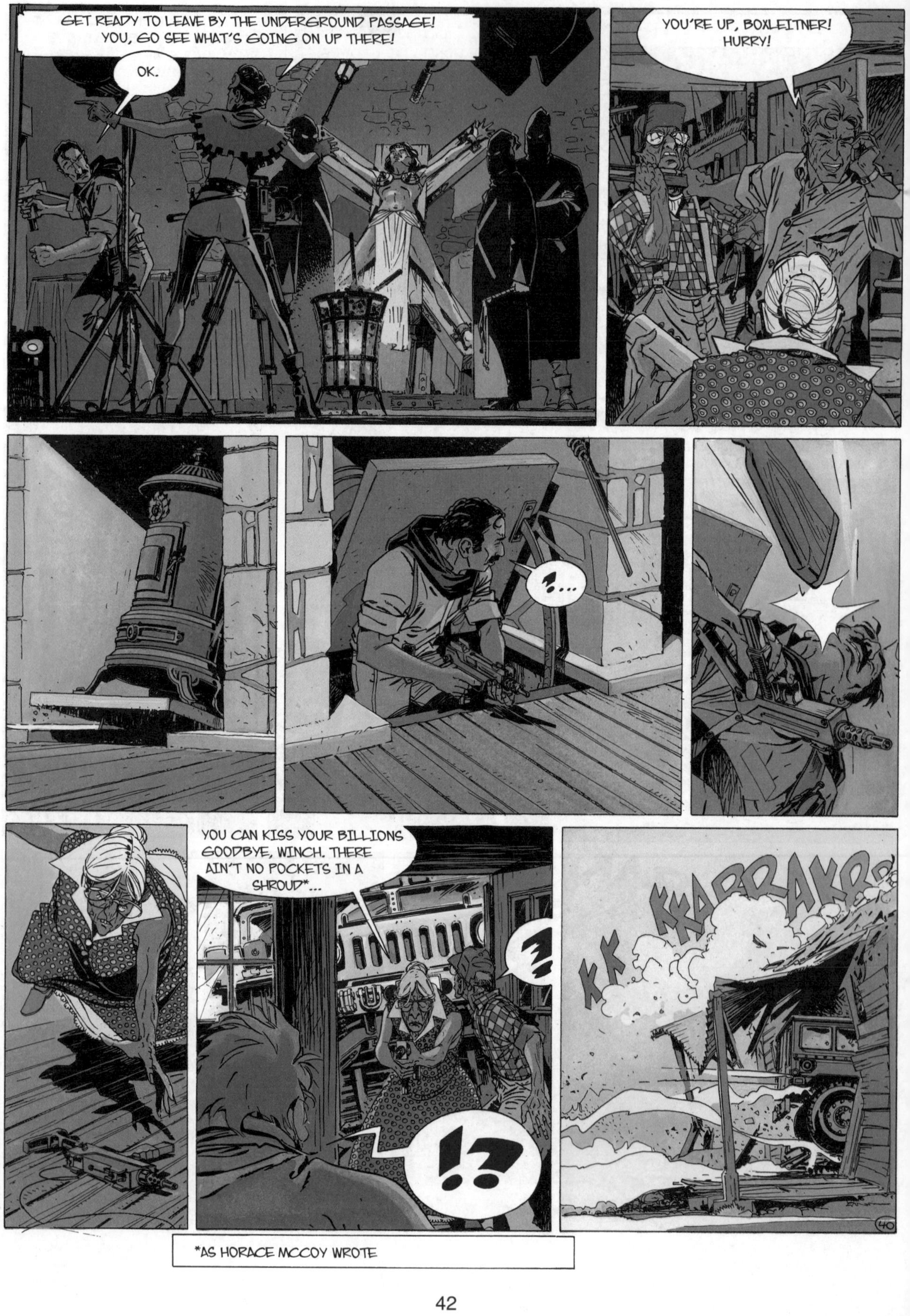

GET READY TO LEAVE BY THE UNDERGROUND PASSAGE! YOU, GO SEE WHAT'S GOING ON UP THERE!
OK.
YOU'RE UP, BOXLEITNER! HURRY!
?...
YOU CAN KISS YOUR BILLIONS GOODBYE, WINCH. THERE AIN'T NO POCKETS IN A SHROUD*...
!?
KK KKARRAKR
40

*AS HORACE MCCOY WROTE

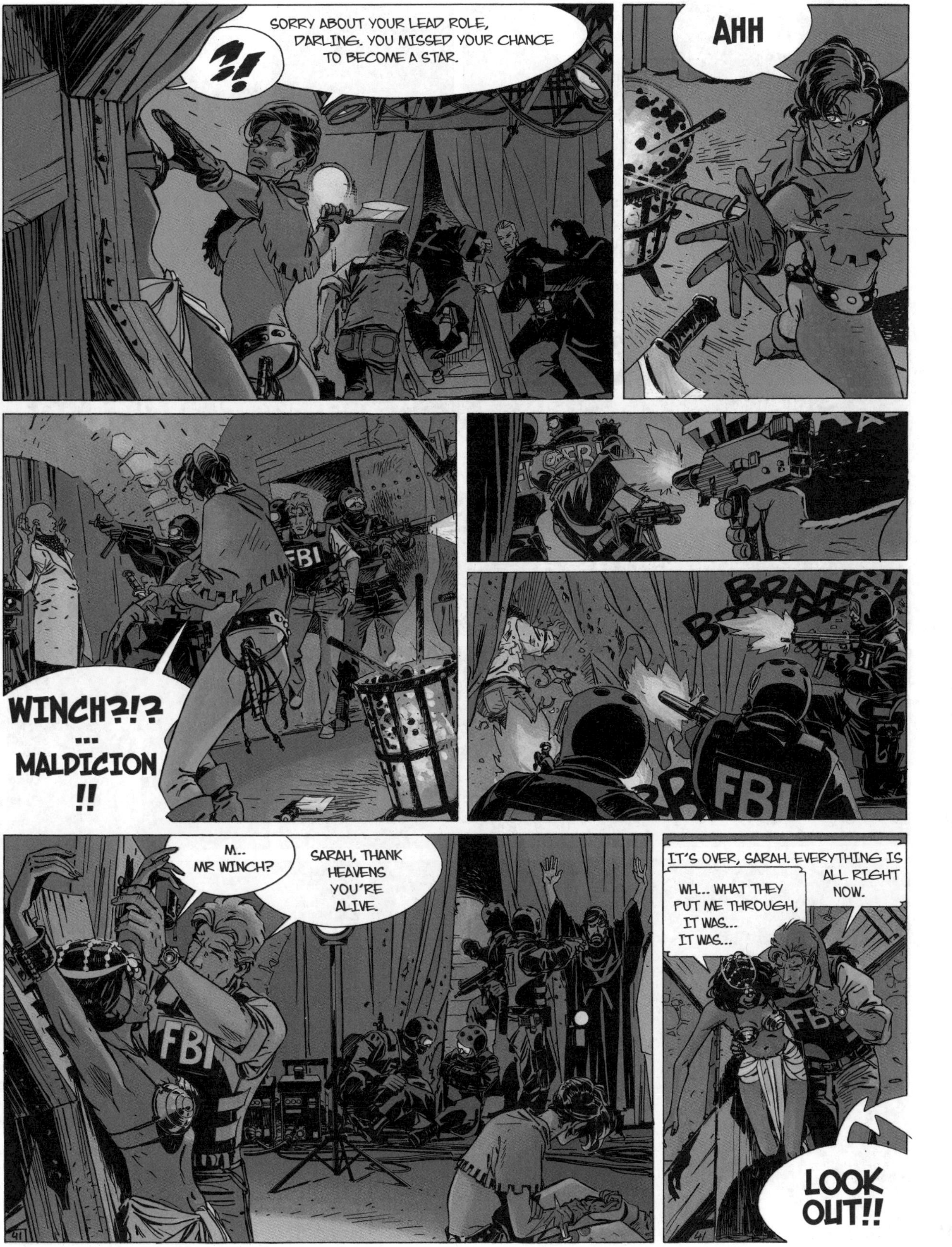
?!
SORRY ABOUT YOUR LEAD ROLE, DARLING. YOU MISSED YOUR CHANCE TO BECOME A STAR.
AHH
WINCH?!? ... MALDICION !!
B-BRAAAA
FBI
M.. MR WINCH?
SARAH, THANK HEAVENS YOU'RE ALIVE.
FBI
IT'S OVER, SARAH. EVERYTHING IS ALL RIGHT NOW.
WH... WHAT THEY PUT ME THROUGH, IT WAS... IT WAS...
LOOK OUT!!

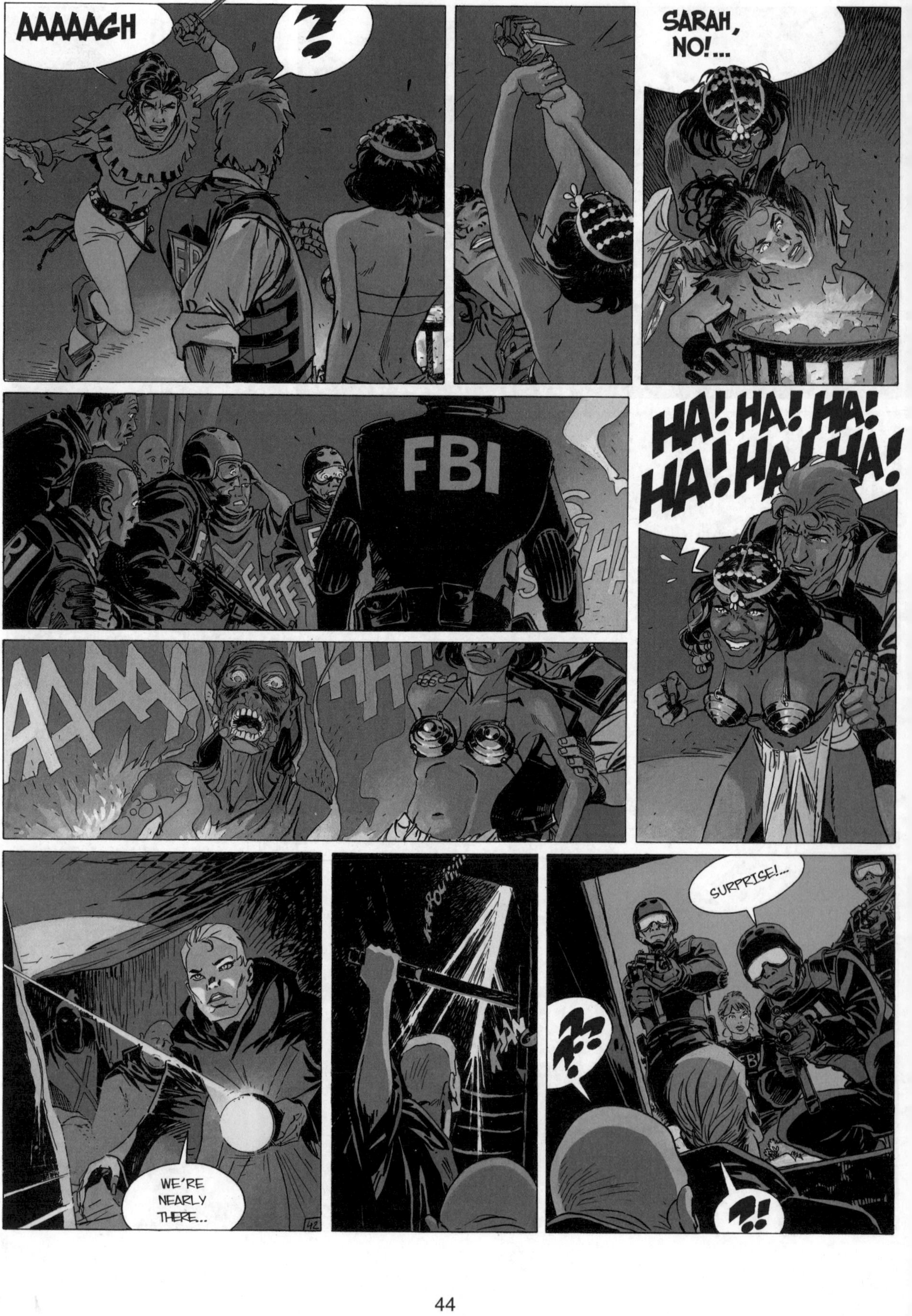
AAAAAGH
?
SARAH, NO!...
FBI
HA! HA! HA! HA! HA! HA!
WE'RE NEARLY THERE...
SURPRISE!...
?!
?!

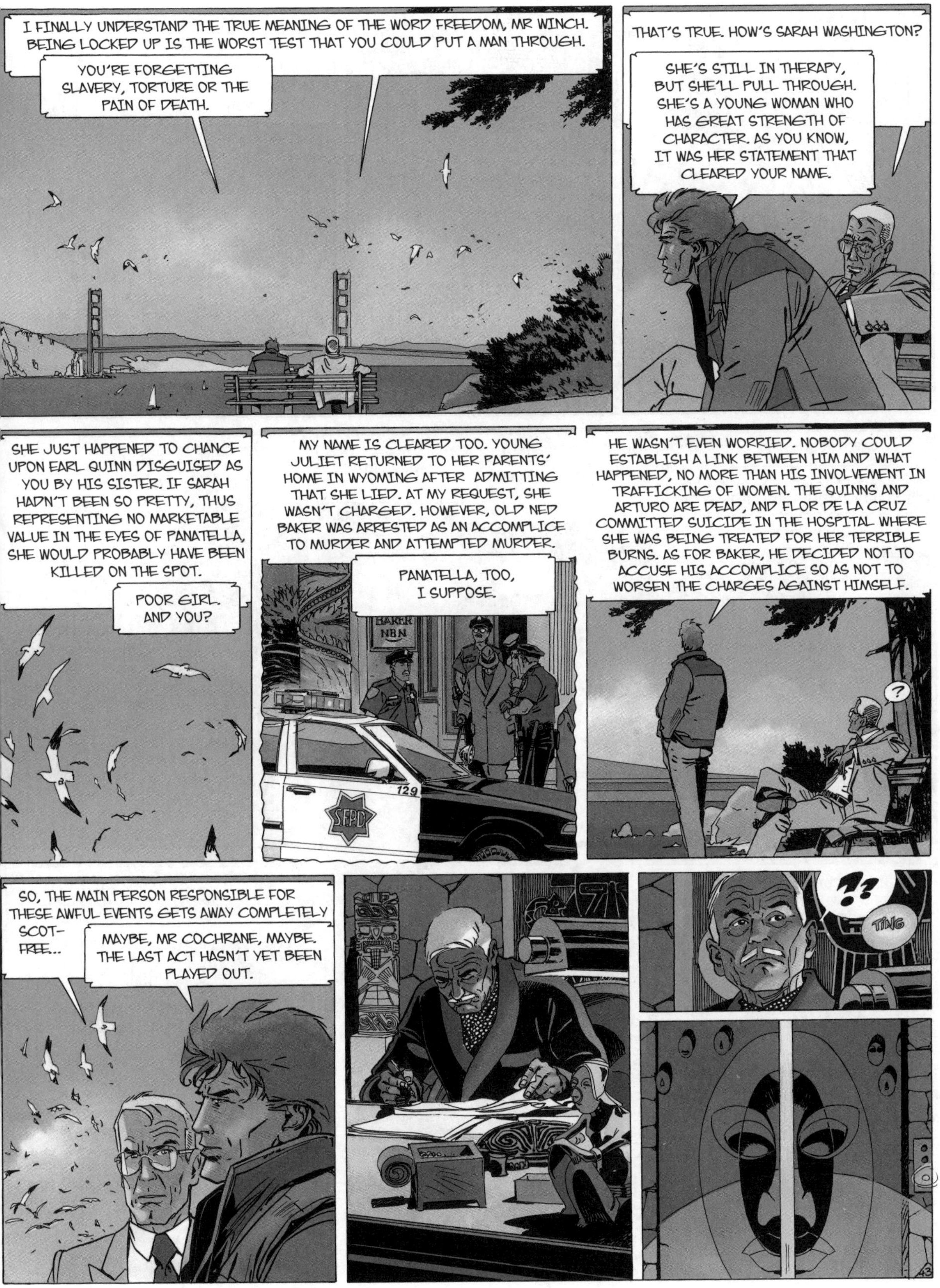
I FINALLY UNDERSTAND THE TRUE MEANING OF THE WORD FREEDOM, MR WINCH. BEING LOCKED UP IS THE WORST TEST THAT YOU COULD PUT A MAN THROUGH.
YOU'RE FORGETTING SLAVERY, TORTURE OR THE PAIN OF DEATH.
THAT'S TRUE. HOW'S SARAH WASHINGTON?
SHE'S STILL IN THERAPY, BUT SHE'LL PULL THROUGH. SHE'S A YOUNG WOMAN WHO HAS GREAT STRENGTH OF CHARACTER. AS YOU KNOW, IT WAS HER STATEMENT THAT CLEARED YOUR NAME.
SHE JUST HAPPENED TO CHANCE UPON EARL QUINN DISGUISED AS YOU BY HIS SISTER. IF SARAH HADN'T BEEN SO PRETTY, THUS REPRESENTING NO MARKETABLE VALUE IN THE EYES OF PANATELLA, SHE WOULD PROBABLY HAVE BEEN KILLED ON THE SPOT.
POOR GIRL. AND YOU?
MY NAME IS CLEARED TOO. YOUNG JULIET RETURNED TO HER PARENTS' HOME IN WYOMING AFTER ADMITTING THAT SHE LIED. AT MY REQUEST, SHE WASN'T CHARGED. HOWEVER, OLD NED BAKER WAS ARRESTED AS AN ACCOMPLICE TO MURDER AND ATTEMPTED MURDER.
PANATELLA, TOO, I SUPPOSE.
BAKER
N.B.N.
129
S.F.P.D.
HE WASN'T EVEN WORRIED. NOBODY COULD ESTABLISH A LINK BETWEEN HIM AND WHAT HAPPENED, NO MORE THAN HIS INVOLVEMENT IN TRAFFICKING OF WOMEN. THE QUINNS AND ARTURO ARE DEAD, AND FLOR DE LA CRUZ COMMITTED SUICIDE IN THE HOSPITAL WHERE SHE WAS BEING TREATED FOR HER TERRIBLE BURNS. AS FOR BAKER, HE DECIDED NOT TO ACCUSE HIS ACCOMPLICE SO AS NOT TO WORSEN THE CHARGES AGAINST HIMSELF.
?
SO, THE MAIN PERSON RESPONSIBLE FOR THESE AWFUL EVENTS GETS AWAY COMPLETELY SCOT-FREE...
MAYBE, MR COCHRANE, MAYBE. THE LAST ACT HASN'T YET BEEN PLAYED OUT.
?!?
TING
43

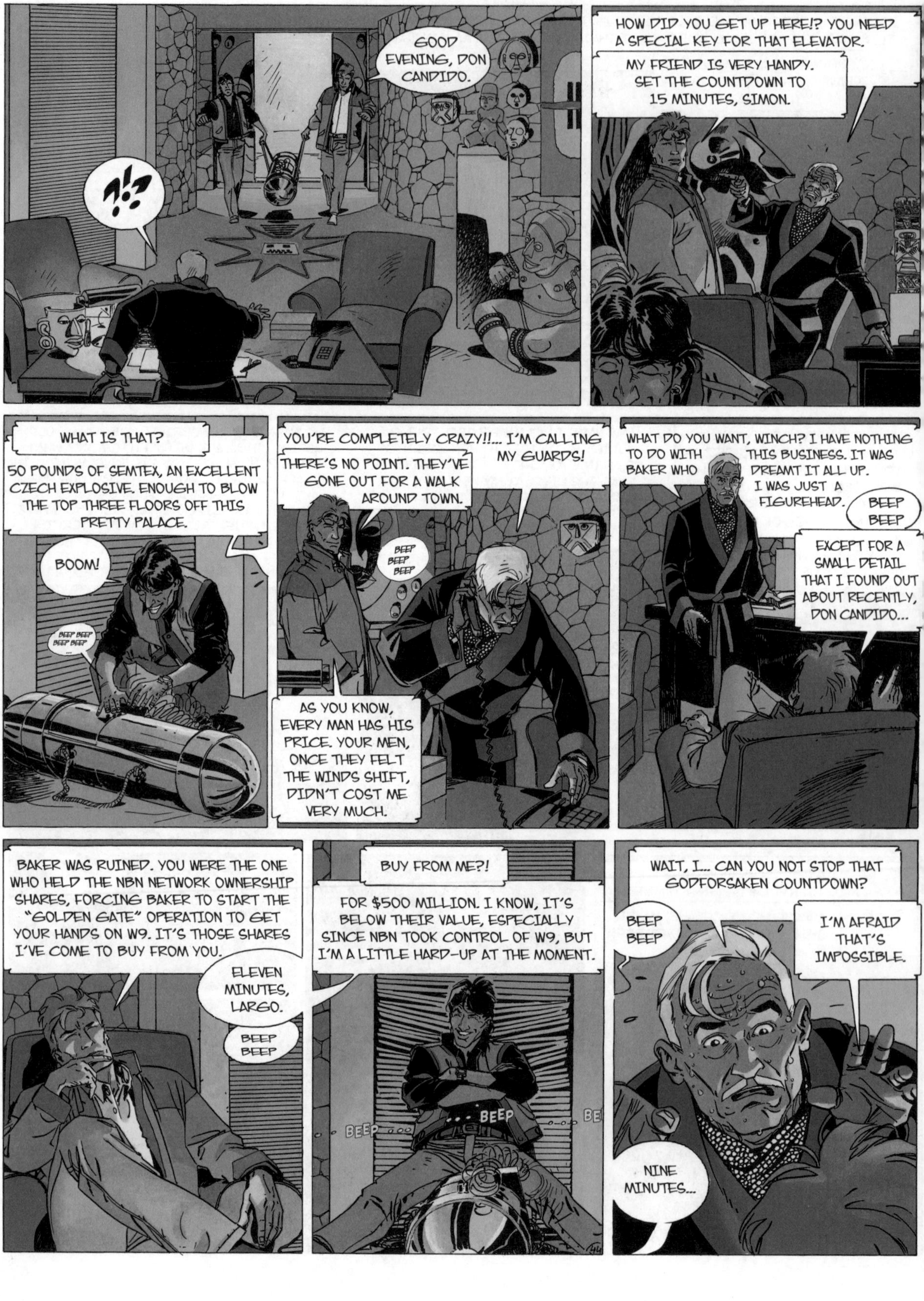
GOOD EVENING, DON CANDIDO.
?!?
HOW DID YOU GET UP HERE!? YOU NEED A SPECIAL KEY FOR THAT ELEVATOR.
MY FRIEND IS VERY HANDY. SET THE COUNTDOWN TO 15 MINUTES, SIMON.
WHAT IS THAT?
50 POUNDS OF SEMTEX, AN EXCELLENT CZECH EXPLOSIVE. ENOUGH TO BLOW THE TOP THREE FLOORS OFF THIS PRETTY PALACE.
BOOM!
BEEP BEEP BEEP BEEP ...
YOU'RE COMPLETELY CRAZY!!... I'M CALLING MY GUARDS!
THERE'S NO POINT. THEY'VE GONE OUT FOR A WALK AROUND TOWN.
BEEP BEEP BEEP
AS YOU KNOW, EVERY MAN HAS HIS PRICE. YOUR MEN, ONCE THEY FELT THE WINDS SHIFT, DIDN'T COST ME VERY MUCH.
WHAT DO YOU WANT, WINCH? I HAVE NOTHING TO DO WITH THIS BUSINESS. IT WAS BAKER WHO DREAMT IT ALL UP. I WAS JUST A FIGUREHEAD.
BEEP BEEP
EXCEPT FOR A SMALL DETAIL THAT I FOUND OUT ABOUT RECENTLY, DON CANDIDO...
BAKER WAS RUINED. YOU WERE THE ONE WHO HELD THE NBN NETWORK OWNERSHIP SHARES, FORCING BAKER TO START THE "GOLDEN GATE" OPERATION TO GET YOUR HANDS ON W9. IT'S THOSE SHARES I'VE COME TO BUY FROM YOU.
ELEVEN MINUTES, LARGO.
BEEP BEEP
BUY FROM ME?!
FOR $500 MILLION. I KNOW, IT'S BELOW THEIR VALUE, ESPECIALLY SINCE NBN TOOK CONTROL OF W9, BUT I'M A LITTLE HARD-UP AT THE MOMENT.
BEEP
BEEP
WAIT, I... CAN YOU NOT STOP THAT GODFORSAKEN COUNTDOWN?
BEEP BEEP
I'M AFRAID THAT'S IMPOSSIBLE.
NINE MINUTES...

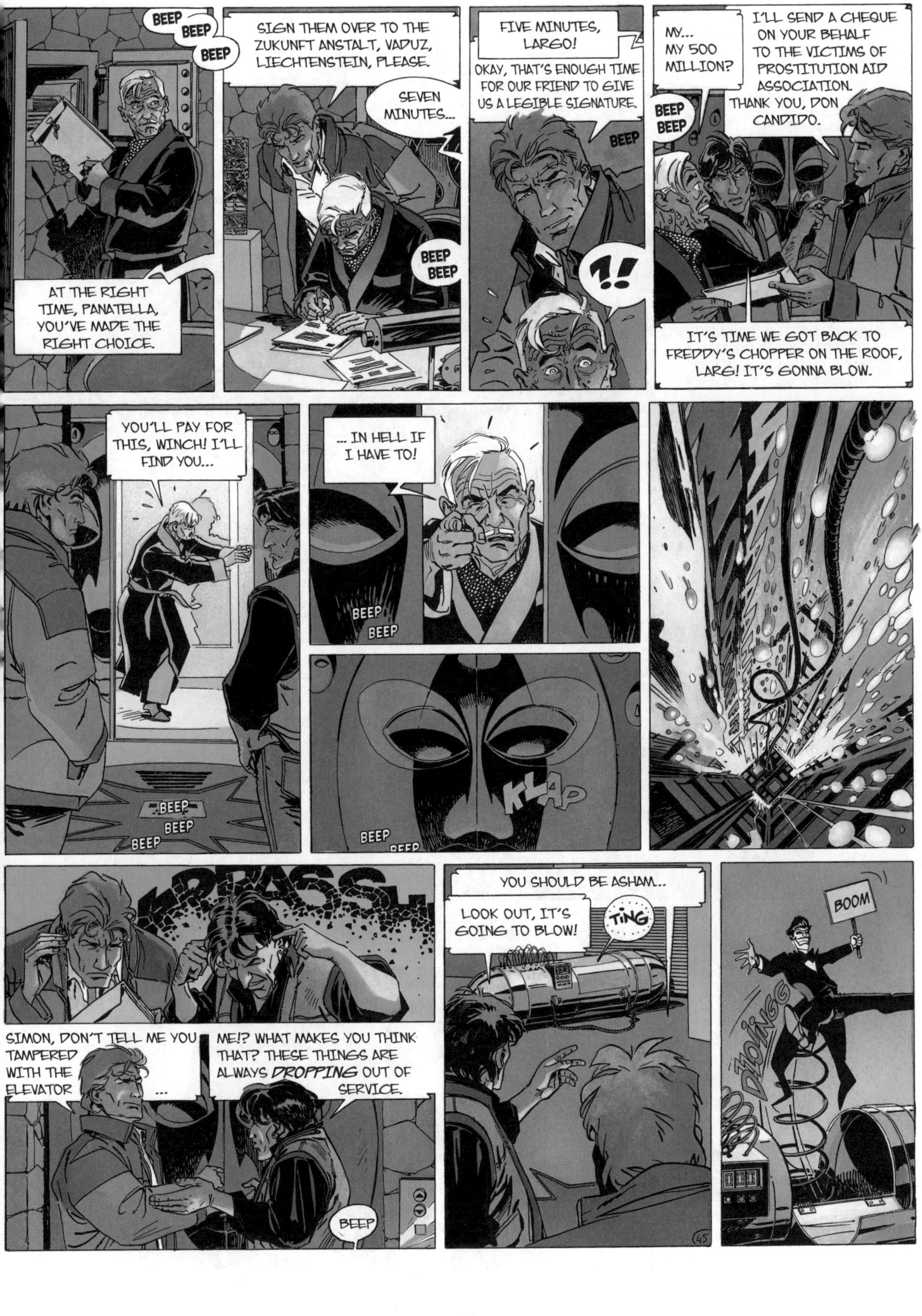
BEEP
BEEP
BEEP
AT THE RIGHT TIME, PANATELLA, YOU'VE MADE THE RIGHT CHOICE.
SIGN THEM OVER TO THE ZUKUNFT ANSTALT, VADUZ, LIECHTENSTEIN, PLEASE.
SEVEN MINUTES...
BEEP BEEP
FIVE MINUTES, LARGO!
OKAY, THAT'S ENOUGH TIME FOR OUR FRIEND TO GIVE US A LEGIBLE SIGNATURE.
BEEP
?!
MY... MY 500 MILLION?
I'LL SEND A CHEQUE ON YOUR BEHALF TO THE VICTIMS OF PROSTITUTION AID ASSOCIATION.
THANK YOU, DON CANDIDO.
BEEP BEEP
IT'S TIME WE GOT BACK TO FREDDY'S CHOPPER ON THE ROOF, LARG! IT'S GONNA BLOW.
YOU'LL PAY FOR THIS, WINCH! I'LL FIND YOU...
BEEP
BEEP
BEEP
... IN HELL IF I HAVE TO!
BEEP
BEEP
KLAP
BEEP
SIMON, DON'T TELL ME YOU TAMPERED WITH THE ELEVATOR ...
ME!? WHAT MAKES YOU THINK THAT? THESE THINGS ARE ALWAYS DROPPING OUT OF SERVICE.
BEEP
YOU SHOULD BE ASHAM...
LOOK OUT, IT'S GOING TO BLOW!
TING
45
BOOM

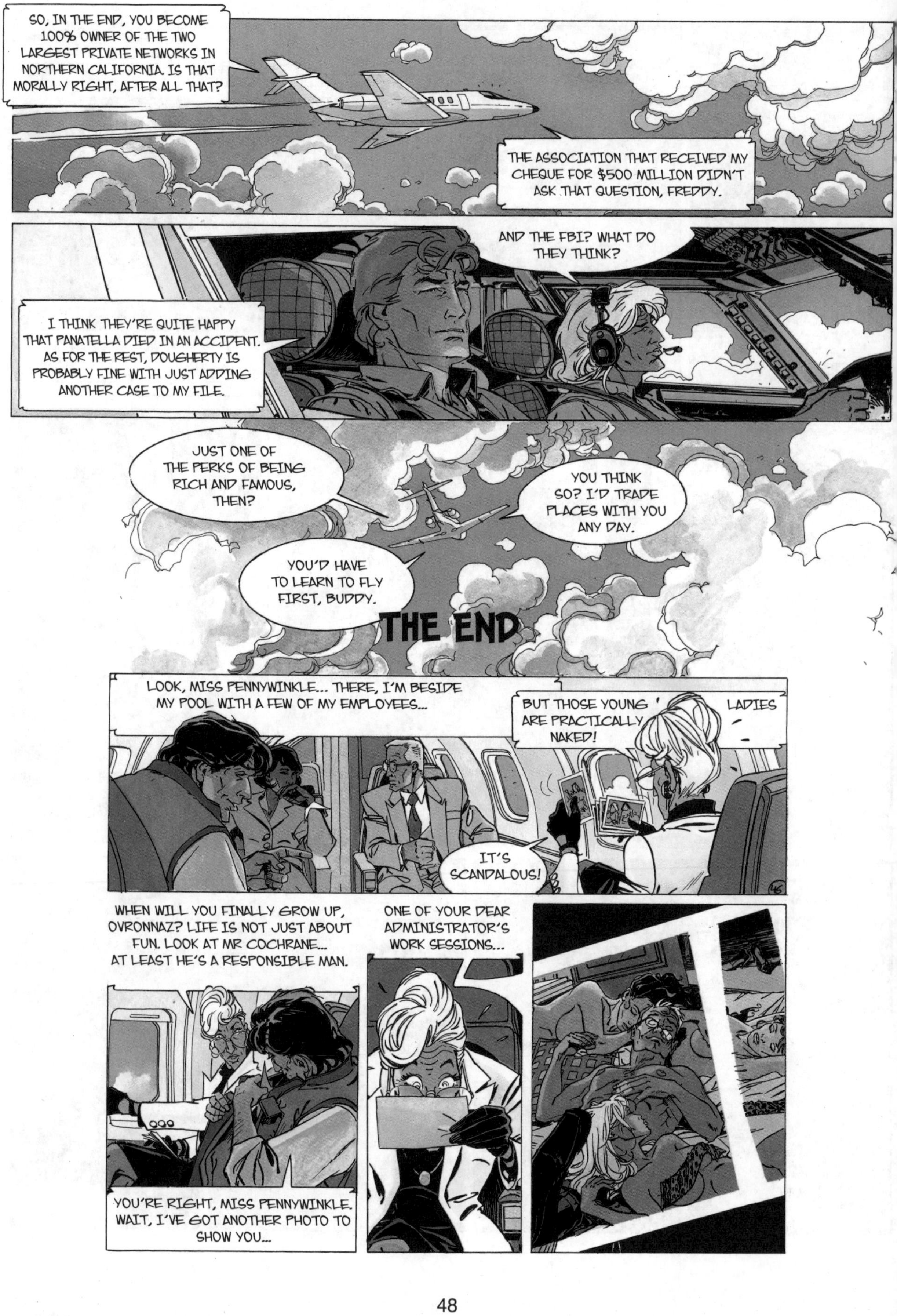
SO, IN THE END, YOU BECOME 100% OWNER OF THE TWO LARGEST PRIVATE NETWORKS IN NORTHERN CALIFORNIA. IS THAT MORALLY RIGHT, AFTER ALL THAT?
THE ASSOCIATION THAT RECEIVED MY CHEQUE FOR $500 MILLION DIDN'T ASK THAT QUESTION, FREDDY.
AND THE FBI? WHAT DO THEY THINK?
I THINK THEY'RE QUITE HAPPY THAT PANATELLA DIED IN AN ACCIDENT. AS FOR THE REST, DOUGHERTY IS PROBABLY FINE WITH JUST ADDING ANOTHER CASE TO MY FILE.
JUST ONE OF THE PERKS OF BEING RICH AND FAMOUS, THEN?
YOU THINK SO? I'D TRADE PLACES WITH YOU ANY DAY.
YOU'D HAVE TO LEARN TO FLY FIRST, BUDDY.
THE END
LOOK, MISS PENNYWINKLE... THERE, I'M BESIDE MY POOL WITH A FEW OF MY EMPLOYEES...
BUT THOSE YOUNG LADIES ARE PRACTICALLY NAKED!
IT'S SCANDALOUS!
WHEN WILL YOU FINALLY GROW UP, OVRONNAZ? LIFE IS NOT JUST ABOUT FUN. LOOK AT MR COCHRANE... AT LEAST HE'S A RESPONSIBLE MAN.
YOU'RE RIGHT, MISS PENNYWINKLE. WAIT, I'VE GOT ANOTHER PHOTO TO SHOW YOU...
ONE OF YOUR DEAR ADMINISTRATOR'S WORK SESSIONS...